"*The Freedom Formula* is not only a practical guide for building a lifestyle business (that makes money) but it's also a kick-in-the-pants to entrepreneurs everywhere to be among the strongest and most positive influences in the new world; a world where everyone experiences real freedom."

~MICHAEL PORT
Author of *Book Yourself Solid* & *Beyond Booked Solid*

"Christine Kloser combines the heart and soul of Mother Teresa with the business savvy of Donald Trump without missing a beat. *The Freedom Formula* gives entrepreneurs both a spiritual road and a practical pathway to build lasting success."

~SUSAN HARROW
Author of *Sell Yourself Without Selling Your* Soul
& CEO of PRsecrets.com

"What a beautiful book! Christine Kloser has written the heart and soul-centered business book the world has been waiting for. With clear examples and step-by-step instructions, she shows you just how to live your life's purpose and make a profit, too. Well done!"

~CHELLIE CAMPBELL
Author of *The Wealthy Spirit* and *Zero to Zillionaire*

"Christine Kloser understands the NEW way of doing business — with heart, soul, love, and plenty of cash to boot! She gives entrepreneurs like us a simple step-by-step plan for true personal FREEDOM. It's how I insist on living my life, and you should too. Don't put off your dreams any longer… get your hands on *The Freedom Formula*."

~ALEXANDRIA BROWN
Author of *Power and Soul*, Marketing & Success Coach and
CEO of AlexandriaBrown.com

"*The Freedom Formula* is a compass that brings forth what is in your soul so you experience the divine gift that is within you. Once you read this book you can't honestly go back to any life of bondage and lack. Real freedom can only come from truth and in your hand you are holding both."

~DAVID NEAGLE
President, Life is Now, Inc.

"*The Freedom Formula* reveals a massively important message…. that bringing your spiritual beliefs into business is the only true path to success. Christine Kloser provides an authentic and powerful approach for combining passion and profit."

~ARIELLE FORD
Creator of EvertyhingYouShouldKnow.com

"Christine Kloser's new book *The Freedom Formula* is a bold step that bridges the importance of 'Soul' in your business. She has weaved the power of being conscious on a spiritual level with the importance of understanding how a business really works. This is a terrific piece of work for anyone who wants to operate a business on a higher spiritual level."

~JOE NUNZIATA
Bestselling author of *Spiritual Selling*

"Finally, a book for conscious entrepreneurs that explains the value of integrating your soul into your business. Christine Kloser makes it clear why advancing consciousness in business is the key to advancing consciousness worldwide - and she makes it appealing, practical and possible."

~JUDITH SHERVEN, PhD AND JIM SNIECHOWSKI, PH.D.
Bestselling authors of *Be Loved for Who You Really Are*

"Finally — someone who brings consciousness and awareness to the business of making money. Christine Kloser takes us on a thrilling adventure of what business could be like if it had both heart and mind. The result is a guide book on how to transform you, your business and the world."

~JAMES ROCHE
"The Info Product Guy," InfoProductGuy.com

THE
FREEDOM
FORMULA®

How to Put *Soul* in Your Business
and *Money* in Your Bank

CHRISTINE KLOSER

Love Your Life
Dallastown, PA

The Freedom Formula®: How to Put Soul in Your Business
and Money in Your Bank

Published by:
Love Your Life Publishing
PO Box 2, Dallastown, PA 17313
www.LoveYourLifeBooks.com

ISBN: 978-0-9798554-4-3
Library of Congress Control No: 2008901177

Cover design, layout and typesetting by Cyanotype Book Architects
Editor: Tara Schiro, Write with Grace
Author Photo by Joe Henson, New York, NY

Printed in the United States of America

Printed on recycled paper.

A portion of the proceeds from the sale of this book will be do-
nated to the charities that Love Your Life LLC supports.

To David and Janet Rose …
the reasons why I want to be
my highest and best self.

LET YOUR BUSINESS LEAD YOU

Let your business lead you.
Let it guide you
to those places in your heart you have yet to discover.
Let it call your soul
to be fully expressed and engaged in the world.
Let it be the way
for you to contribute your unique gifts to the world.
Let it be your tool
for making the planet a better place.
Let it be your vehicle
for leaving a legacy long after you are gone.
Let it be YOU…
…mind and body, heart and soul.

~ CHRISTINE KLOSER

C O N T E N T S

FOREWORD

Is it possible, even feasible, to incorporate spirituality into your business and still be able to build a highly successful enterprise? Most definitely yes!

Some people would laugh at such a concept, but I've been saying for quite some time that business, and the way you do business, is your highest spiritual understanding demonstrated.

It is in business and commerce where the world will turn toward a new idea about itself because nothing turns the wheels of life faster, or more consistently, than business and commerce. Ever it has been and ever it will be because the way we interact with each other, the way we transact the business of life, is crucial to the experience of the creation of life itself.

I want to emphasize that there is no such thing as a separation between business and spirituality. It's time to stop disintegrating yourself, because in so doing you disintegrate life itself. To understand this key principle and the important process of recreating ourselves anew is to understand it begins with the recreation of the way you do business, the way you undertake commerce. So this is a vitally important topic for you to understand because... business IS your highest spiritual understanding demonstrated.

In this book, Christine Kloser beautifully explains how to integrate your spiritual nature with proven business principles to become a successful, conscious entrepreneur. Christine's unshakable belief in operating her businesses according to her highest spiritual understanding, has led to the creation of this straightforward spiritual approach to business... for the purpose of having YOUR highest spiritual understanding demonstrated, and positively impacting the world through your business.

If you've been searching for a way to enrich your business by adding the spiritual essence of who you are, trusting in your Divine plan, and cementing your connection to your Source AND your clients, then keep reading.

You'll enjoy the journey!

NEALE DONALD WALSCH
Author of *Conversations with God*

A CKNOWLEDGEMENTS

As in any undertaking in life, it takes a tremendous amount of support to birth a book. There are so many people to thank for the contributions they made to me, both knowingly and unknowingly as I walked through the experience of bringing forth this book.

To God, who has gifted me with so much to be grateful for and has given us all a Divine spark of light that can never be extinguished, no matter what. This book would never have been brought to life, had You not assisted me in writing every single word. Thank you.

To all of my clients, customers, mentors, mastermind colleagues, newsletter subscribers and the hundreds of women who were members of NEW Entrepreneurs, for being the mirrors that show me who I am. And, to all my circle sisters on both the west and east coast, especially Ami, Jen, Felicia, Debbie, Mary, Deb and Kathryn, your support is with me every moment of every day.

To Laurel, Kamila, Sierra, Bonnie, Peggy and Terri for

being the beta-testers of *The Freedom Formula*. The impact you had on this book finally coming forth is profound. Thank you all for helping the floodgates within me to open and come forth on my keyboard.

To my husband David, who was the first one of us to proclaim, "I'm going to write a book." If you never stepped up to the plate to write your book, my journey into publishing would never have begun. Thank you for following your dream, and always supporting me in the pursuit of mine... and ours. I love you.

And, to our daughter Janet Rose. Thank you for choosing me to be your Mom. You truly are God's greatest gift of all.

And, finally, to the spirit of the child I miscarried in 2006. Your short presence in my life is a blessing beyond words. Losing you was the catalyst that caused me to re-evaluate everything and make new decisions that lead to the writing of this book and the rapid transformation of me, my business, and my life. I miss you and I'll never forget you.

PREFACE

Thank you for allowing this book to come into your life at this exact moment in time. As with everything you've ever experienced, this book being in your hands right now is part of your Divine plan.

After reading the prior paragraph, either you'll think I'm crazy for speaking of your Divine plan in the context of a business book or you'll be captured by my words because they resonate with your soul. If the latter is true, you've probably been looking for confirmation that the desire to blend your business aspirations with your spiritual beliefs and principles IS the right way for you to BE in business.

You can take a refreshing and relaxing deep breath now. You have found your home in this book. You're not alone in your desires to integrate these two worlds (Spirit and business); in fact you are part of a growing number of conscious entrepreneurs who view their business as the perfect vehicle for their highest self-expression in the world... their freedom.

Throughout the book, sometimes I'll refer to God, and

when I do I'm not pointing to any particular religion. I'm referring to the Universal Source of unseen energy that exists in and around every living thing; the Source that causes and sustains life in all shapes and forms. I personally refer to this energy as God. But, if the word God doesn't resonate with you, replace it with whatever word feels like a fit for you. The important matter is for you to get the information in this book, because you attracted it to yourself for a reason. So, if that means replacing the word God with Energy, Universal Flow, All That Is, Source, or anything else, that's OK with me. Do what works for you!

My intention in your reading this book is that it'll have a transformative effect on you, your clients and customers, your family, your friends, your health, your Spirit, your relationship with God... everything. For, God, truly is your ultimate business partner and the Source in which all things come to you. It's time to bring that energy more presently and more fully into your business... and your life. After all, there is no separation between your spirituality, your business and your life; it is all ONE. We are all one.

Enjoy the journey...

Christine

I N T R O D U C T I O N

Thank you for picking up this book, and reading it! One thing I know about you already is you're a business owner/entrepreneur (or want to be). The other thing I know about you is that you place FREEDOM very high on your priority list. In fact, you'd likely give up security and stability for the freedom to pursue your dreams and live the life you feel destined for.

In addition to wanting freedom, you are also a very spiritual being. Your spiritual beliefs and understandings form a strong foundation for your life. And, while you may not meditate or pray everyday, you believe in a power much greater than yourself. No matter where you go, or what you encounter, you trust there is an Order to everything; and everything you experience falls under that Order one way or another, including your business.

Aside from a couple of great books that integrate spirituality and business, there isn't much information being published on the topic. It's easy to find books about business, and books about spirituality, but it is hard to find books that combine both topics under one cover. I personally needed a 'manual' for how to bring spirituality into my business—not just my life—in an ongoing basis. When I couldn't find this manual anywhere, I set out to create one and thus *Freedom Formula* was born.

In reality, the concept for *The Freedom Formula* was probably born the moment I hopped in a 1987 Volkswagen Fox with two girlfriends after I graduated college. I was moving 3,000 miles away from my home in Connecticut to pursue a new life in Southern California. Although I wasn't aware of it at the time, my quest for freedom had begun. I felt called to create a new, fulfilling, exciting and purposeful life. So, I went as far away from that old 'normal' life as I could... without having to leave the country! Thankfully, my life defies any picture of normal; rather, I've designed it to work for me! And that's what *The Freedom Formula* is about... a life (and a business) that works for YOU spiritually, financially and emotionally!

The Freedom Formula is the culmination of 15 years of entrepreneurial experience, ongoing personal development, continual spiritual evolution and my insatiable curiosity (fellow Sagittarians will relate to that). I have been bringing together the concepts in this book for nearly 20 years, without ever realizing they were being gathered for the purpose of writing this book. It's interesting to me, considering that this is my fourth book (the first three were from my *Inspiration to Realization* anthology book series), that I haven't dealt directly with this topic. But now it is time and all these years of experience have been distilled into a simple formula, *The Freedom Formula* which looks like this:

$$(S + C + D + I) \times E = F$$

and stands for this:

$$(\text{Soul} + \text{Connection} + \text{Design} + \text{Implementation}) \times \text{Energy} = \text{Freedom}$$

Don't worry. It'll make a lot more sense by the time you finish this book.

My quest to achieve personal freedom and spiritual expression combined with having an intense curiosity lead me to interview and/or host seminars and events for more than 100 leading experts on the topics of business and spirituality. I wanted to learn everything I could from well-established, conscious and very successful entrepreneurs; not only for myself, but to share their wisdom with you as well. Some of the experts I've worked with include:

- Neale Donald Walsh, Author, *Conversations with God*
- Michael Gerber, Author, *The E-Myth*
- Martha Beck, Columnist for *O, the Oprah Magazine*
- Seth Godin, Author, *The Dip*
- Dr. Joe Vitale, Author, *The Attractor Factor* and featured in *The Secret*
- Michael Port, Author, *Book Yourself Solid*

- Marcia Wieder, Author, *Make Your Dreams Come True*
- Kendra Todd, Winner of *The Apprentice* and Author, *Risk and Grow Rich*
- Loral Langemeier, Author, *The Millionaire Maker* and featured in *The Secret*
- Joe Nunziata, Author, *Spiritual Selling*
- Susan Piver, Author, *The Hard Questions*
- Alexandria Brown, Author, *Power and Soul*
- And many, many more.

Each interview I hosted and each event I produced helped me take the next step along my journey. Each one helped me discover more of who I am; each one put me on the path that lead to writing this book. Here, in these pages, I've brought together what I've learned, discovered and created for myself, my business, and my clients... so that you, too, can experience freedom in your life.

But, before you dive into this book, I'd like you to take a few moments right now to think about the word freedom and what it means to you. It's a word that means many different things to different people. And, for the purposes of this book, the only meaning that matters is yours.

To help you with this exercise (and all the exercises in this book), I've developed The Freedom Formula action guide. It's my gift to you so you have one place to gather your thoughts and ideas as you move through the information in this book and further along your Divine path.

Please download and print your action guide now by going to **www.TheFreedomFormula.com/guide**

ACTION GUIDE EXERCISE #1

Write down your definition of freedom as it pertains to your business.

www.TheFreedomFormula.com/guide

Another practice that will help you immensely in reading and applying this book is to find a "book buddy" to read (and do) the book with you. Together, you'll hold each other accountable to complete the book and action guide while supporting one another to implement *The Freedom Formula* into your business and your life.

This book isn't just a book to read. It is meant to be studied, experienced, shared and used as an exercise that furthers you on your journey of conscious business success. To get the full impact of the transformation that lies ahead for you in the following pages, please engage yourself fully by downloading the action guide and partnering with a book buddy now. I promise your journey will be worth it. Even if the clouds above you may appear gray, the journey you're embarking on is a blissful one; there is always a blue sky above the clouds, and a Divine light shining within.

Come now; let's begin your exciting journey of putting soul in your business and money in your bank!

Love and light,

Christine

Discover The Soul of Your Business

(Soul + C + D + I) x E = F

Every business has a soul; an energy that exists inside the business that permeates every aspect of the entity and the impact it has on the world. It's the essence of the business; the "thing" that makes your business unique, glorious and a perfect piece in the Divine Order of the Universe. It may be a new concept for you to grasp that your business is a significant element to the Order of the Universe. But, it's true.

Each business exists as an energy, much like each human being exists as an energy; each fulfilling it's part in the world. Each part, no matter how small it may seem when viewed as part of the Universe, is significant. This includes you and your business. Here's an example that'll help you get a feel for this.

Think about the interior workings of a clock (not a digital one, but one with hands that tick). The clock has a number of gears inside, each one doing its exact job to make sure the clock works. Now, each of those gears has numerous teeth that are necessary to keep the gears going as they're supposed to. If one of those teeth isn't there; the clock won't work. No matter how many other gears and teeth there are, if just one of them is missing the whole system is out of whack.

It's the same way with the Universe, when you consider that every living being is one of those teeth; every one is a piece of an integrated whole. So, if you ever doubt that your business is a significant element to the Divine Order of the Universe, think again. You and your business are a necessary piece of a much greater whole.

I can't claim to fully understand the power of this unseen Universal energy I call God. Perhaps one day when I make my transition, I will have a deeper understanding. But for the purposes of this book, it's important to share that I absolutely believe there is an energy that exists outside of us that has everything to do with everything. It is the ultimate Source of all that is, and it is always there, no matter what. This energy cannot be turned on or turned off; there is no beginning or end to its supply. It simply IS.

Can I guarantee that this is 100% truth? No. But it serves me to BELIEVE it is. Think about it. What is the alternative? To go about your life, and your business, believing it (and you) exists completely separate from everything else? That you are not connected to anything outside of yourself? For me, that would be a horrible existence; to believe there isn't some higher order to our lives, and that we are not connected by one unified Source. So, I choose to believe. I choose to accept this Energy (God) as true for me. And, I can tell you that once I fully accepted this as true for me, and tapped into the unseen energy that is right there in front of, within, and around me every moment of every day… everything changed.

Your job as a conscious business owner is to allow this energy into your business and your life; to let it flow through you and guide you in your endeavors. As I said earlier, the energy is always there, and can never be "turned off." The only thing that can be "off" is you. If you feel the energy flow is blocked, it is not about the energy, it's about you. Sorry to be so direct about this, but it's an important concept for you to grasp.

Somehow, someway, perhaps by simply allowing it to slip from your conscious awareness, you may feel disconnected from that Source. But, don't worry. It hasn't gone anywhere, and a simple shift in your awareness can bring the connection back. *The Freedom Formula* is designed to help you maintain that conscious connection and allow it to guide you as you take steps to create the business and life you've always dreamed of. Because when you're living your life connected to God's abundant energy, and consciously connected to the Universal flow of All That Is, your soul can be fully expressed in the world and you can BE who you were born to be.

The Soul of Your Business is…

By now, you may be asking, "then, what IS the soul of my business?" The answer is simple. The soul of your business is… you.

As a business owner, your soul IS the essence of the business. You are the person who birthed the business. You are the person whose creativity brought forth your products and services. You are the person who has a vision and takes steps to realize it. You are the person who believes your business is a vehicle to make a difference in the world, and to be part of the positive evolution of life as you know it. So, you see? The soul of your business is... you.

But, sometimes after a few months (or years) of being in business, you may lose sight of that initial excitement and connection. Perhaps your business faces some difficult challenges. Maybe you are discouraged that clients didn't flock to you immediately. Perhaps the money you had to start your business has run out. Maybe you're downright tired. All of these are situations that can arise in business. But, there is something you can do in times like this.

You can hop off the treadmill of continuous action and allow yourself to remember why you started your business in the first place. Now is the time to reconnect with the spark within you that feels called to create, contribute and cause positive change in the world. *The Freedom Formula* is a journey anchored in the conscious awareness of every aspect of you, your business, the world around you and the abundant Universal energy.

ACTION GUIDE EXERCISE #2

Take a moment to write down the reasons why you started your business.

www.TheFreedomFormula.com/guide

The 4 Components of Conscious Business

Seeing that the key element we're talking about here is increasing your conscious awareness, it's a good time to talk about the elements of being a conscious business owner. This isn't anything I learned when I earned my Bachelor's degree in Business Management, and it's certainly nothing I learned on a tele-seminar or by reading popular business books. I've come to this definition through my personal experience and feeling drawn to integrate my spiritual nature into my business.

There are four criteria that make up a conscious business. I invite you to review these aspects of your business and engage in an honest and purposeful evaluation of where you stand on each of these components:

Component #1:
A Conscious Business Makes Money

This was a very difficult concept for me to embrace. Like many conscious entrepreneurs, I cared a lot about my customers and clients; sometimes more than I cared about myself. I had been willing to sacrifice my own needs to help others and I'd give away my time, my knowledge, my ideas, everything... without asking for anything in return. I wanted to be of service, and to help as many people as possible. So I did it at all cost—and it did cost me a bundle— because I didn't want to let anyone down. For that wouldn't be a conscious business, would it? Ha!

Sometimes it's challenging to combine your desire to "serve" with the desire to make money. Is it really possible to combine Mother Teresa and Donald Trump? Yes. I know these two energies feel like they go together as well as oil and water. But, in order to be a successful and profitable conscious business owner you need both. Money is simply a form of energy that is exchanged for the service you provide to the world. You deserve to be well compensated for that!

I believe that in order for our world to survive (and thrive) through these rapidly changing times, it needs for you, the conscious entrepreneur, to make a lot of money so you can spread more of your wisdom, love, knowledge, heart and soul out into the world… giving back in a BIG way!

If you looked up the definition of "business" in Webster's dictionary, you'd see something that says business is "a profit-seeking endeavor." If you do not seek, and realize, a profit, it is not a business. It is a charity, it is a sinking ship, it's something you'll begin to resent and dread because the lack of money drains every ounce of energy from your being. It's a great challenge to elevate to the higher energetic vibrations of Source energy when you don't have enough money for rent. I know because I've been there.

I had built a business on my desire to connect with and be of service to like-minded women entrepreneurs. Money never entered into the equation until I found myself knee-deep in owning a full-fledged women's networking organization. While it appeared to be successful on the outside, I knew the truth. The business wasn't even breaking even. I had to support the business with my own money.

From what members told me, my networking organization was one of the most powerful groups they'd ever experienced. It brought spirituality and business together in the same space. I loved and cared about the members, and I know they loved and cared about me, too. All of my events for this organization were a "love fest." Women would leave the monthly meetings feeling deeply connected to each other, to themselves, to Source and to their vision for their business. Often times, the hotel banquet manager (where we met) had to kick us out of the banquet room at 11:30 at night, nearly two hours after the meeting had ended! Nobody wanted to leave, especially me! I wanted to drink in every ounce of energy from that conference room.

So, you can imagine the gut-wrenching decision I had to make to shut down the organization. Why? The more I explored the concepts of conscious business, the more I realized my networking organization was an UNconscious business. Because when it came to the financials, I had been operating with blinders on… I was scared to face the truth. How could I run a failing business while taking a stand that making money was a core component of a conscious business? I couldn't. So I took my own advice and shut down the business. It was one of the hardest things I've ever had to do. It helped that I gave "departing" gifts to each and every member of the organization with a value that far exceeded what they had paid for their membership. So, my conscience was clean, which helped ease my personal sadness and feeling of letting down the members.

Making the choice to use my profit-and-loss statement

as a guide to determine the close of that business (when my heart told me otherwise) said to the Universe that I was serious about making money. This action in the physical world, along with my willingness to do something that was extremely uncomfortable for me, was a very clear signal that something had shifted within: that I was ready and felt worthy of receiving a lot more money. And, I did.

I'm not asking you to shut down your business, but I am asking you to increase your awareness of the financial health of your entity. One of the best ways to do this is to spend some time reviewing your profit and loss statement. Look at the numbers to see if what you're doing is really working in terms of money. When you love your business, and your clients, it can be very challenging to look at your business in a "black and white" way. But, it is necessary. Let's face the music here. A business that doesn't make money, isn't a business at all… it's a hobby. This book isn't about hobbies; it's about putting soul in your BUSINESS and money in your bank.

While we're on the topic of money, let's quickly clear something up here. You are meant to attract a lot of it. Not for the purpose of acquiring material possessions and being able to keep up with the Jones'. Instead, you're meant to receive a lot of money so you can keep up with your soul's desire to be fully-expressed in the world (more on that later). Trust me, that plan is not for you to be in survival mode for the rest of your life.

So whether you make $50,000, $500,000 or $5,000,000 per year, now is a good time to look at the bottom-line of your business.

ACTION GUIDE EXERCISE #3

It's time to review your gross revenues, income, expenses, debts, and profit to see if your business is trying to tell you something.

www.TheFreedomFormula.com/guide

You may want to put on some relaxing music, light a candle and make yourself a cup of tea while you look at the numbers of your business to see and hear what they are saying. The numbers can actually speak to your soul because they'll guide you towards making decisions. Decisions that'll help you make more money, be more fulfilled, and experience more joy in your business.

Component #2:
A Conscious Business makes a difference.

The second component of a conscious business is to make a positive difference in the lives of others. A company that produces and markets a diet pill that is known to cause damage to the human body is not a conscious business. But, the consultant whose deepest commitment is to transform their clients' lives, and quite possibly the world, by sharing their knowledge and wisdom, is a conscious business owner. Thankfully, there are many thousands of businesses that already operate under this context of conscious business. I'm sure you have experienced a few yourself aside from your own business.

For instance, if you have a carpet cleaning business it might not seem like it's making as much of a difference as an alternative medical practitioner who restores her patients back to health. But, here's the truth. Carpet cleaning does make a difference in the lives of the people who are having their carpets cleaned. It's helping them live the kind of lifestyle they want to live. It's keeping a cleaner environment for their family. It's keeping a home where the homeowners are eager to open up their doors and invite in neighbors and friends and loved ones to enjoy space and time in their home.

So a carpet cleaner, when you look at it close enough, truly is making a difference to their customers and clients. This should be the thing you keep in mind the most when you're working with a new customer or talking to one of your clients. It's truly connecting with the concept of how you can be of service to them, and how you can positively impact their lives. When you're operating as a conscious business owner, it's not just about closing a deal; it's about being of service and making a difference.

Occasionally this will mean you'll refer your prospect or client to somebody else, if that referral can better match the needs of your client. Because, when you truly want to make a difference by serving your prospect or client as best as you possibly can, it might not always mean you are the best one to help them. This can be a very difficult concept to swallow. Let me give you an example to illustrate how this works.

Last year, I was talking with a potential joint venture part-ner. We'd been going back and forth for months on this deal that we're trying to put together. Last week he asked me something about one of my publishing company's "competitors." (I put "competition" in quotes because I don't believe in the concept when talking about it in the context of a conscious business... more about that in component #3.) Rather than panicking I said, "I really appreciate that you asked me about this and here's how our services are different." Make note that I didn't say mine were better, just different.

After explaining the differences very-matter-of-fact I said, "But I understand as a business person, if you do your research with them and find that they're a better fit for you, it's perfectly okay with me. I want you to work with the person that you are meant to work with; the person with whom you are divinely meant to do this project with. If it's me, fantastic; I am grateful to move forward with you. If it's someone else, then I've really enjoyed getting to know more about you, and working with you on the possibility of this project. I'll wish you well. If ever down the road my services might come in handy again, please let me know. I'm here to help."

I couldn't believe I actually said this, and really meant it. This was probably the biggest deal I've ever worked on in my life, and I was completely detached from the outcome. I trusted that whatever unfolded for both of us would be for our highest and best good.

This is what I'm referring to in this second component of making a difference. It's when you are committed to making such a difference that if you, or your prospect's highest good is going to be served by not doing business together, you wish them well in working with a different company. In this light, you are truly being of service... to the Divine plan. The space that opens up for new possibilities will surprise you by bringing you more of what you do desire, and more of the right clients for you. The saying is true; when one door closes, another door opens.

This can be a very scary place to enter, especially when you feel like you "need the money." It is much easier to do when you believe 110% in yourself and your product or service, and you don't have any doubt about what you can (and cannot) provide your clients. The increased confidence you get from believing in yourself and your business is a necessary piece of being willing to go to these places to make a difference.

The other aspect to consider is not only in making a difference for each individual customer or client, but also connecting with the difference that you want to make in the world. How will your business positively transform others? What is the legacy you want to leave? How will your conscious business make the world a better place? How will you best serve the evolution of our society?

ACTION GUIDE EXERCISE #4

What is the difference that your business makes in the world; what is it contributing to the overall whole?

www.TheFreedomFormula.com/guide

These are the questions to ask yourself to remain connected to the specific difference you make in your daily interactions with others and the world at large.

Component #3:
A Conscious Business Calls You To Be Fully Who You Are

If you've ever felt like you had to hide a piece of yourself in your business, it's not a conscious business. Rather, a conscious business draws forth every ounce of your spirit and calls you to be more of who you are. Your conscious business needs you to be who you are because that is exactly where your success lies.

Too often, business owners feel like they "should" be a certain way in business, and a different way in life. It's just not true. The only way to succeed as a conscious business owner is to be ALL of you, all the time. The very qualities and characteristics that make you, you, are the exact qualities and characteristics your business (and customers and clients) need you to be.

It's incredibly challenging to put on your "game face" while trying to fit into someone else's idea of who you should be. Or, worse yet, your own misguided idea of who YOU think you should be. The joy truly comes in surrendering to exactly who you are…. yes, every tender loving ounce of your being; quirks, idiosyncrasies and all. Those are the things that make you who you are, who God meant for you to be the moment you were born.

One side benefit of being fully who you are in your conscious business is that you have no "competition." Nobody can be you. Nobody can duplicate your heart and soul. Nobody can exude you, but you. So, as you discover and express more of your essence, the more you distinguish yourself in an overcrowded market of entrepreneurs who are trying to be someone else. In so doing, you will only attract those customers and clients who are meant to work with you. You become a natural magnet for your best clients.

As we discussed in the second component, sometimes you may be the one to refer your client to someone else if they can be better served elsewhere. But, how do you know if they're not the right fit for you? The answer is simple. If you feel yourself being compromised by actively pursuing the business, or you feel your dream becoming further out of reach, it's not the right fit. You'll know when this is happening because you won't feel called to be more of who you are; you may even feel like you're making yourself be less just to get the business. Watch out for this pitfall, it can ruin you and your business.

The moment I was willing to let go of this potential joint venture, the experience (in and of itself) literally called forth more of who I am. It allowed me to share a part of myself that hadn't yet been shared in a business relationship. So, the simple act of letting go of the idea, in the presence of my prospect, allowed this component to come to life within me and my business. It allowed me to experience more of who I am.

That's what made it okay for me to tell my prospective joint venture partner I would support him working with my "competition" because they really aren't my "competition." It was simply that the other company's highest expression may be a better match for my client's needs. So, let's look at the flip side of this. If I tried to convince this prospective partner to work with me and did whatever it took to close the deal, I would've had the experience of being less than "who I am." I'd have had to compromise something to try to be that which I am not. This doesn't serve anyone.

Because, being who you are is the strongest asset you can have as a business owner. The "secret formula" of you can never be knocked-off. And, oh, what fun it is to discover that your most important role in your business is to be more of your Divine self. How lucky you are that this is your highest mission in your business, and your life. How blessed you are that deep down inside you probably already know this. Perhaps right now you're even nodding your head "yes" in thankful agreement that you get to discover and share more of yourself through your business. Awesome, isn't it!

So, I invite you to be the glorious being you are. Embrace everything that feels easy, natural and graceful. It's these very things that guide you to experience more of yourself. While these experiences that are most natural to you may not seem like anything spectacular, they are in fact everything. They only seem like nothing to you because you're blind to seeing that which is innately who you are. Success is supposed to be easy. When you're simply being you and doing all that comes naturally as your Divine self, success flows.

ACTION GUIDE EXERCISE #5

Identify your natural gifts.

www.TheFreedomFormula.com/guide

Component #4:
A Conscious Entrepreneur Trusts In Their Divine Plan

The fourth component of conscious business success is to trust in your Divine Plan. This means to always know, no matter how challenging, no matter how much a particular client might be driving you up the wall, no matter how much you're pulled off track, that you continue to step forward in every moment and trust that your Divine Plan is perfectly unfolding in your life. And, you do this without panicking when negative emotions start creeping in.

One of my clients asked, "What do I do when I feel lack or doubt coming into my mind and my Divine Plan is nowhere to be seen?" The answer is simple, but not necessarily easy in the moments of distress. And that is to reconnect back to Source energy. When you feel negative emotions rising within you, it's time to make a conscious shift away from the dark, downward spiral of the those emotions. You do this by elevating your awareness to the vibration of God/Source. By doing this it makes it easier to realize that the experience you're having is literally a "blip" in relation to the Divine Plan for your life. It is this elevation of consciousness that allows you to see the Divine

Plan so you can surrender to it, and know that "all is well."

There are a myriad of ways to reconnect with Source and rediscover trust in your Divine Plan. We'll cover a few of them in the next chapter. But, one of my favorite methods to shift my vibration and embrace trust in my Divine Plan is to listen to guided meditations. This is a tool I have and continue to use in my life, and I'm convinced that guided meditations were my saving grace when I experienced some huge challenges in my prior businesses. So, I've made it easy for you to take advantage of this same tool. I've recorded a meditation for you to download immediately at **www.TheFreedomFormula.com/guide** It's called, "Trust in Your Divine Plan" and it'll gently guide you back to your trusting heart and peace of mind.

Please take some time today to download and listen to this guided meditation.

Action Guide Exercise #6

What is your Divine Plan?

www.TheFreedomFormula.com/guide

Believe me, you don't want to miss out on this powerful meditation. Normally, the cost to download the meditation is $19.95, but because you're reading this right now, you can download the meditation absolutely free. Consider it my gift to you, so you always have a way to rediscover the trust in your Divine plan.

How Are You Doing?

Now that you know the four components of conscious business success:

1) Make money; 2) Make a difference; 3) Be fully who you are; and 4) Trust in your Divine Plan, it's time for you to do a self-assessment.

Take a moment right now to honestly assess how you're doing in each of these four criteria:

1. My business makes money
   ___Yes   ___ No
2. My business makes a difference
   ___Yes   ___ No
3. My business calls me to be more of who I am
   ___Yes   ___ No
4. I trust in my Divine Plan
   ___Yes   ___ No

Please, do not use this assessment as a tool to judge yourself. There are no right or wrong answers. This is meant only to be a vehicle for elevating your awareness (becoming more conscious), of where you stand in this moment of time as it pertains to you, and your conscious business.

If you didn't say "yes" to every criteria, but wish you could, that's OK. Just having this realization means you are much further on the path than you were before you cracked open the cover of this book. Now you know the areas that need your focus, intention and attention.

What Were You Thinking?

We can't address the concepts of consciousness and aware-ness without also exploring the influence your thoughts have on your reality because every thought, intention, idea, image, feeling, experience, success, failure, opportunity and challenge have brought you to where you are in your life right now. Of this entire list, however, your thoughts and intentions are the most powerful. When you begin to fully comprehend that your thoughts and intentions create your reality, you'll see that where you stand today is a culmination of all of your past thoughts.

Don't like what you see from where you stand right now? It's because of the thoughts that have persisted in your past. And, that's good news! Why? Because the more aware you become of the power of your thoughts, the easier it is to create your future.

Everything that's occurred in your past to cause every thought you've had… has divinely directed you to now. And, now is such a beautiful moment because it is where all future creation begins. While we're talking about the beginning, let's go back to your beginning in this life.

When you were born you were closely connected to the Divine; you were born as a radiant being, filled with light, love, grace, acceptance, and a deep connection to the Spirit that brought life forth through you. At the moment of your birth, there was no fear, doubt, scarcity, lack, or wondering if you were enough. You just were. And, you were more than enough. You knew with your first breath you would always be okay because the Source that created you would always be there.

But, along the way, you forgot what you knew then. You learned from others who lost sight of the Divinity within them. You were told what was right and wrong, told what to believe and not believe. Maybe you were taught to believe that money was the root of all evil, that you should be seen but not heard, that you shouldn't believe in "pipe dreams," that you had to work hard to make money, and that financial success was the only measure of a person. It's unfortunate these thoughts were projected on you, most likely both consciously and unconsciously. The good news is now you get to think your own thoughts, and eliminate the old thoughts that no longer serve you. You are at the helm of your own life; you are the director of your own thoughts. So, it's time to reframe some of your old programming.

For instance, money isn't the root of all evil, it's the source of good in the world (when it's in the right hands); your voice should be heard loud and clear and never squelched; in God's eyes you were born to fulfill your "pipe dreams" (after all they were given to you by Source); money comes to you not through laborious work but the inner work of being fully who you are in the world. You are not measured by the amount of money you make or things you acquire, but by the joy you experience and spread in the world (and, yes, money makes this part much easier... which is why it's so important to make it).

Just in case there's a single cell in your being that's thinking, "It's not spiritual to be rich…" listen up one more time! You absolutely, without a doubt, were born to have money. The only way to be fully expressed as a conscious entrepreneur (not a hobbyist) is to have the freedom to engage in the experiences that allow you to discover more of yourself, and to express yourself through your growing business. And, that takes money!

Conscious entrepreneurship is about making a positive, lasting impact on the world… through your business. You have a message to share, valuable information that can change people's lives and you want to reach the 'masses.' The reality about fulfilling this vision and dream is that it takes money to grow and sustain your business at this level of success. You need systems, structures, marketing and a team in place to help you do all this. So, money is a necessity in order for your business to make its greatest contribution. Certainly, if you have the desire for a profitable, expansive conscious business… you also have the ability to manifest everything you need to realize this dream. Money, included! Yet, keep in mind, one thing money cannot buy is happiness. Happiness is a state of mind you can experience anytime, anywhere.

That being said, however, money *can* buy you leverage. It makes it possible to hire the right people to handle the tasks you don't enjoy doing; you're freed up to do what you love. Money allows you to buy more education and travel to meet colleagues who can help you grow your business. Money makes it possible to put systems and structures in place that make your business run even when you're not there. Money buys leverage, and leverage gives you more freedom.

Let me just pause to say that there are amazing people who have done, and are doing, incredibly valuable work in the world and making a massive impact without being wealthy (just think of Mother Theresa). But, this book isn't written for charities or missionaries. We are talking about conscious entrepreneurship. So, that is the context in which I emphasize the importance of you receiving and leveraging money to help you achieve your dreams.

OK, so we've gotten clear about what constitutes a conscious business. And I trust since you're reading this right now that you're "on board" with this way of doing business. So, let's explore a bit more about this first step in The Freedom Formula; discovering the soul of your business.

Your Multi-Faceted Life

Seeing that the soul of your business is YOU, you can't proceed any further without taking a look at every facet of your life right now. You see, your business is only one facet of your life, although sometimes it feels like everything. The truth is your business is a reflection of EVERY area of your life.

That being said, it's time for you to take an inventory of your life. The interesting thing about this inventory is that all of these areas are integrated into the one (and only) life you will live in this physical body. So, you're not looking at these areas to identify points of separation, you are looking at all of these areas of your life to seek threads, themes, consistencies, unity and ultimately a fully integrated picture of your life.

Following is a list of the areas of your life you'll be assessing. For each of these areas, when asked, please write about:

1. Your current experience in that area;
2. Your level of emotional satisfaction in that area;
3. Your challenges in that area;
4. Your highest vision in that area.

You'll do a lot of writing during this exercise, which is a good thing. The more clarity you have about where you are now (and not just in your business) the more power you have in transforming your life and achieving new dreams. Clarity IS power.

ACTION GUIDE EXERCISE #7

Answer the above four questions as a discovery tool for a full, personal, life assessment, as they pertain to the following areas of your life.

www.TheFreedomFormula.com/guide

Your Life Assessment

*   Personal (health, relationships, family, recreation, hobbies, etc.)
*   Spiritual (your connection with the God of your understanding)
*   Financial (your overall financial health and wealth)
*   Business (the vision, operations, staff, system, plan, marketing, delivery, etc.)

What's Working For You?

Before you go another step further, it's important now to clearly identify what is working (and what isn't working) for you. It's time to look at your inventories and note those areas that are going incredibly well, also noting those areas that bring the most dissatisfaction and stress. (There's space in your companion guide to write about this, too.)

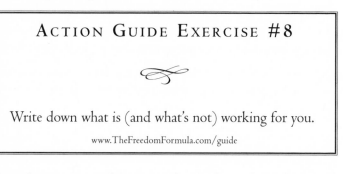

ACTION GUIDE EXERCISE #8

Write down what is (and what's not) working for you.

www.TheFreedomFormula.com/guide

From here, you can begin to release what isn't working and focus on what IS working so you can begin to live your highest vision. Something to keep in mind as you reflect on those things that may need to be released is this: if it's not working for you, it's not working for God either. In God's world, you are meant to experience joy, and do that which feels natural and easy. These natural and easy experiences are the ones that bring you closer to the Divine and closer to the full expression of you.

But, let's face it. Joy can be pretty far out of reach when you find yourself continually bogged down taking action on tasks that drive you nuts. Every entrepreneur can relate to this. You can tell by the way you FEEL if, on one hand, you're stuck in dead-end details, or if you're doing something that really "lights you up."

Shorten Your 'To Do' List And Lengthen Your 'To Be' List

So, let's figure out what "lights you up" so your emotional state rises to the higher, more positive emotions where creativity, abundance, opportunity and joy are a limitless experience!

The way you'll do this is by bringing a new perspective to your "to do" list by filtering it through a four step process. This is a great way to discover more about where you are, and begin to put more soul into your business, by eliminating those things that drag you down.

ACTION GUIDE EXERCISE #9

Answer the questions and follow the steps ahead, using the Action Guide as a space to write the answers.

www.TheFreedomFormula.com/guide

What you'll see there are five pages with these headings written on the top of each page:

1. Current "To Do" List
2. For Someone Else
3. Get Done Later

4. Not Worth Doing
5. "Light me up" tasks

First, take a few minutes to write down all of those items on your current "to do" list. Simply think about different aspects of your life (including business, of course) and write a laundry list of everything that you do. This can be an overwhelming task, so take a few deep breaths and know that as you get more clarity about where your time and energy are being spent, you can begin to take control of how you want to purposefully invest your time and energy to achieve your dreams; rather than simply doing what's in front of you because it's there to be done.

Once your list is complete, begin to categorize each task by asking yourself these four questions. Once the answer is clear, write that task on the appropriate page.

1. Can someone else do this task, instead of me? If so, whom?
   -Write these tasks on your "for someone else" page.
2. Can this task get done later? Nothing is as urgent as you think.
   -Write these tasks on your "get done later" page.
3. Is this task worth doing at all? Some tasks don't matter in the long run.
   -Write these tasks on your "not worth doing" page.
4. Is this a priority for you? Will it bring you joy, and more money?
   -Write these tasks on your "lights me up" page.

Now, I realize that executing this four step plan for each and every task may be a stretch for you. Especially if you're new in business and don't have someone to delegate to yet. In that case, I suggest you seek out an intern from your local community college or hire a local stay-at-home mom for $15 per hour. Do whatever it takes to get someone on board to handle some of the details. Begin to get rid of annoying tasks by delegating the things that drive you most crazy. It's not a good thing to do things that make you want to pull your hair out!

Here's something to keep in mind as you get other people to help you with those things you hate doing. The people who help you with those tasks love doing them. I know it was difficult for me to comprehend that someone actually liked handling the details for me. But, my assistant would tell you herself that she absolutely loves it. Here's the beauty in this... not only do YOU get to express more of your highest self by doing those things that "light you up," but those people that help you get to experience more of their highest self, too. It's a win-win situation that just can't be beat.

The ultimate purpose of filtering your tasks through this four step process is for you to shorten the number of items on YOUR priority "to do" list. Why? Because when your "to do" list gets shorter, you have more space to "be;" your "to do" list is now comprised of tasks that bring you joy, tasks that "light you up." So, you experience more of who you are meant to be by only doing these things that bring you joy. Yes, you get to BE more joy, more love, more fulfillment, more light, more expression, more connection, more peace, more of everything. And, this is the place where everything flows so your dreams can be realized more quickly and easily.

Let Go... to Soar

I'd like to issue a mild warning here. Through this process of assessment, evaluation and self-reflection in discovering the soul of your business, you may find you're someplace you don't want to be. You may be years into a business (or a piece of your business) you don't want to be in. Perhaps you've invested thousands of dollars into a strategy that isn't working.

Do yourself a favor. Take a deep breath right now and trust that all is unfolding in Divine perfect order, even if this is bringing up some negative emotions or fear about what to do. If this is your current experience, please understand that this, too, is part of your Divine journey; that the very experience of discontent or confusion is an essential piece to get to clarity and joy.

So, if you find yourself (like I did) knee-deep in something that isn't working, you have one of two choices to make. Quit or keep going. Seth Godin's succinct book *The Dip* talks about this concept beautifully. Sometimes it makes sense to quit and sometimes it's worth sticking out what Seth calls "the dip." FREE GIFT: Listen to my interview with Seth Godin, where we talk about "The Dip" and how to know if you're in one. **www.TheFreedomFormula.com/guide**

You'll need to spend some time assessing your particular situation to determine if you forge forward or not. If you choose to let something go, it's imperative that you don't attach yourself to it as a failure. Every "failure" is simply a new understanding, a new insight, a new wisdom, a step to a new and better endeavor.

I shared earlier about the pain I went through in letting go of my networking organization, the Network for Empowering Women; but, let me tell you, the experience I gained and who I became as a result of that experience, was one of the most critical pieces to where I stand today. My current business could never have grown like it has, if I held on to the dead weight of a financially unsound business endeavor. Please keep this in mind if you're going through a release in your business. You're not alone, it's been done before and if it's truly the right thing to do, you'll be amazed at what transpires through your act of courage in letting go.

It's time to give up any lingering conversation about having to struggle or pay your dues. It's an irrelevant concept. Your job now is to vibrationally (energetically) match that which you want and desire.

The Best Frog Is The Leap Frog

We can't talk about being a vibrational match without talking about the concept of leap-frogging. This concept was first introduced to me by my friend, colleague and mentor, Alexandria Brown. It's a concept that eliminates the old corporate paradigm of ladder climbing; the concept of having to "pay dues" or "work hard and struggle" to get ahead.

Leap-frogging, in my opinion, is a spiritual practice. It's about placing yourself in an emotional state of vibration above that which you feel right now. For instance, if you're a $75/hour coach and feel comfortable with that rate, you would leapfrog by doing the inner work to enter the vibration of being a $250/hour coach, if that's what you desire.

There isn't any law that says you have to work hard or climb ladders to get ahead. The Universe says, 'even before you ask I will have answered.' So, what you're asking for is already there for you, and you'll see it when your thoughts and emotions are aligned with your highest intentions. What I mean by that is, if you say you want to be a $250/hour coach and feel like a fake when you say it, then, of course, the Universe cannot deliver on such a misaligned intention.

So, your real job in "leap-frogging" is doing the inner and outer work of having your thoughts and emotions fully resonate with what you say you want. This, my friend, is the path of the conscious entrepreneur. It's a continual evolution in your awareness, your expression, your thoughts, your intentions and your connection to the unlimited Source that provides you everything you desire. In truth, it is already there waiting for you to claim it.

I'll share a quick story about my personal experience in learning how to "leap frog." It was at my 2006 Conscious Business Retreat where I'd be reintroducing myself as a conscious business coach after taking a few years off to start my family.

When I had stopped coaching in 2003, I charged $350 per month for three 60-minute sessions. After all, that was what I saw most other coaches doing, so I figured I would do the same thing. But now that I was reintroducing my coaching services, $350 per month just didn't resonate anymore. So I began the journey of developing my new programs and rate structure. I took into consideration my life, the value of my time, the types of clients I wanted to work with and then created a coaching offering that met all of my needs.

When I crunched the numbers and honestly assessed what my rate should be, I nearly fell over. My calculations (based on Dan Kennedy's formula to determine the value of your time, page 27 of *The No B.S. Guide to Time Management*), was $500/hour. Since I had designed a coaching package that included 10 hours of my time, it meant the fee should be $5,000; a far cry from $350 for 3 hours.

I experienced quite a challenge saying $5,000 without coughing, or justifying myself as soon as I said the price. So, I spent a lot of time meditating on the number, talked with a few coaches and colleagues about it, and did a lot of inner work to come up with a fee less than $5,000 but still felt like a big stretch to me... and felt like I deserved it. I knew I hit the right mark when I sold out my first 5 coaching days in 48 hours at a $3500 fee. So, this first big leap I took was to charge $3,500 and in less than 1 year, I leap-frogged up to $5,000 per day. And, I don't cough at all when I say it.

I believe that if I had set a fee that didn't resonate with me, I wouldn't have sold out right away. The Universe would have known I had thoughts of doubt, fear, unworthiness, etc.; which is why this process doesn't work without the spiritual aspect of resonating with what you say you want. It only works when it's right for you on every plane. Don't worry if it takes you a while to make your first big leap. The good news about leap-frogging is that after you've done it once, it gets easier to leap again and again and again.

Be Here Now

Everything you've learned in this chapter is about getting to the soul essence of your business, the soul of you. It's about having clarity on where you stand right now in this moment of time. You simply can't get to your destination (your dreams) if you don't know where you're starting from. A sure-fire way to post-pone your success is to skip this important step of discovery. There's a reason why the first element of *The Freedom Formula* is this discovery process of putting soul in your business. Nothing can happen without it.

If you glazed over (or ignored) the exercises in this chapter, now's your time to go back and do them. This is your opportunity to discover what you need so you can experience the reality of your soul-filled success.

Connect to Your Source... and To Your Market

(Soul + Connection + D + I) x E = F

Once you've gone through the steps in the previous chapter (to discover the soul of your business, and gain clarity about where you are), now it's time to make the connections needed for your success. So, the 2nd step of *The Freedom Formula* is to connect, connect, connect.

As you probably noticed, the title of this chapter is about connecting to your Source, AND to your market. Only in a book about conscious business can I talk about connecting to your Source and your market in the same sentence. The reason why I've combined these two topics into one chapter is because you need to have both of these connections operating simultaneously if you're going to realize long-term, sustainable success in your business.

The integration of the tangible and intangible, spiritual and practical, visible and invisible parts of your business and your life are the foundation for your conscious business success. Without the integration of these two worlds, there is no Conscious Business.

Many conscious business owners unfortunately focus on one aspect or the other. They're either very focused on their market (and their marketing) or they're focused on their connection to Source and their spiritual evolution. Just recently, a colleague of mine admitted she had basically dismissed her spiritual practice for nearly 6 years in pursuit of her business and marketing goals. After some deep reflection, she realized she needed to embrace both sources of connection in order to experience her highest self, and more success in her business. And, she hesitates to think about what her business would have been today, had she not given up on her spiritual path all those years.

Chances are that you lean toward connecting to one aspect more than the other. So, let's identify what your natural tendency is by taking a look at which one of these scenarios resonates most with you. Keep in mind as you read the following scenarios that this is not an exercise in judgment; it's an exercise to become more aware.

Please pick the scenario that most resonates with how you live your life now:

Scenario I: You are busy from the moment you wake up to the time you go to sleep. You hit "send/receive" a dozen times a day and find yourself consistently feeling that you have to "do more" because you're always "behind." You're excited about the prospects of marketing your business and getting more customers… and more money. You haven't meditated, journaled or enjoyed any spiritual connection on a regular, daily basis and you keep wondering when it's going to get easier.

Scenario 2: You are deeply enmeshed in your spiritual journey, and sometimes it consumes you. You don't feel particularly motivated to take practical action in your business, and procrastination feels like your middle name. You feel very connected to your Source/God and would rather spend time on your spiritual pursuits than implementing a marketing plan.

Once you've identified which scenario is most like you, you'll clearly see if you lean more toward your spiritual nature or your practical/business nature. Again, this contemplation isn't to make room for judgment, but simply to bring more awareness.

Conscious business is about both aspects of your business, so if you're serious about being on this journey, which I trust you are, you'll find it worth your energy to bring more balance into embracing both energies outlined above: the "take action in the physical world" energy AND the "spiritual evolution" energy.

The reason you need to embrace BOTH aspects in your business is because no matter how connected you are to Source, no matter how much you meditate, pray, visualize and intend... if your goals and dreams are not connected to the "real world" and the market you serve then there is no vehicle for your Divine gifts to be received, and, vice versa. If you're consumed by the concrete tangible aspects of your business and your market (and leave your spiritual life at the curb), you're missing out on the most powerful resource of all.

Seeing that your Divine gifts were given to you for the purpose of sharing them with others, it's safe to say your gifts are not supposed to remain your "best kept secret." And, the fastest way to unlock YOUR secret is to allow yourself to be a conscious conduit of connection to both worlds. *The Freedom Formula* refers to this second step as being connected to Source and to your market.

Your Connection To Source

By this point you may be asking how you can connect more deeply with Source. And, how do you KNOW when you are consciously connected and when you're not? Let me remind you that you are ALWAYS connected to Source, but sometimes you forget. Sometimes your conscious awareness of this connection has completely slipped away. So, how can you maintain this conscious connection to Source?

Here's where the distinction of opposites comes in handy to make a point because it's easy to identify when you are disconnected from God. You're disconnected when you experience feelings of fear, struggle, doubt, lack, scarcity, even hate. It's when life feels hard and you allow yourself to be pulled down by your reality on the physical plane. Since you believe in an unlimited, abundant Source that is the pure essence of love, then the presence of negative emotions can be embraced because you know they are there for a reason. They serve as guideposts to make you aware that your connection to Source is temporarily turned "off"... and that you have the power to consciously turn the flow of that Source back on.

When I was nearly forced into bankruptcy from a previous business failure, (not the Network for Empowering

Women, but a yoga studio) I spent a lot of time being aware of the fact that I felt completely disconnected from Source. I woke up nearly every day in a panic about money. How was I going to pay rent? How would I pay my staff? How would I get through to the next day? I remember a particularly challenging moment when I had to scrape up dimes and nickels to buy a $.99 burrito so I could eat dinner. I can feel my heart sinking and tears forming in my eyes as I reflect on that time of my life.

Did I know God's Divine light was shining on me during that time? Yes. And yet, it was extraordinarily challenging to get through the day from one moment to the next. But, let me share with you the moment when everything started to change, the moment I turned "on" my conscious connection to Source.

I had just finished a conversation with a bankruptcy attorney because I felt that was the only way out of the darkness I was experiencing. I remember sitting on my bed with the phone in my hand, and my husband sitting at the foot of the bed with me. I hung up the phone, and cried for a good long while. Then, through my tears of doubt and pure terror, I began to sense the goodness in the situation. In my moment of despair, somehow I was able to grasp the idea that this, too, was happening for a reason; a Divine reason that would reveal itself to me over time.

This sense of connection to Source quickly began to ease my burden. I embraced this feeling of absolute knowingness that "all is indeed well" and I lifted my eyes, looked at my husband and said, "I don't think we should file for bankruptcy." He was shocked because our situation was so grim, but I spoke with him about this feeling I had and the absolute knowingness that we were meant to figure out how to thrive, and not just survive through this ordeal.

I felt that if I filed for bankruptcy it would be an easy out from having to step into the life I had always envisioned for myself. Instead, I chose to figure out a way (with Divine guidance) to use every ounce of this experience (and the wisdom I gained) to catapult me into a whole new realm of business... and being.

Please let me say this was the right choice for me. I understand that many people chose to file bankruptcy (perhaps you or someone you know) and that is the right choice for them. I'm not sharing this story to make a statement about bankruptcy; I share it to make a point about the depth of the moments that can bring about a deeper connection with your Source.

And, please remember that not all of these moments of deeper connection come from a negative experience, many times they come from the most joyous experiences of your life. I'm sure that as you reflect on your own life, you'll remember your personal moments of embracing a deeper connection with Source.

Maintain Your Connection

So how do you maintain this connection consciously and continually at deeper and deeper levels? That's a good question, and one I trust you'll be on a quest to answer until you leave your earthly body. I believe that one of your highest purposes in this experience of life on earth is to become closer and closer to that Source. I think it's one of the very reasons why you were born; to remember back to the divinity you knew at your beginning. That being said, I'm going to do my best to share some insights on how to maintain this conscious connection.

Before I do so, let me first say that in your journey of connecting with Source, there will be moments where you feel it profoundly, and times when you don't feel it at all. This is natural and part of your evolution.

Some moments when you feel it the easiest may be when you hold a new baby in your arms, relax in nature, dance, make love, attract your perfect client, experience a deep connection with a good friend, or look into the adoring eyes of a child. I refer to these as my "woo-hoo" moments. You may have this experience too; when life is so in the flow that you have to holler out loud, "woo-hoooooooo!"

My neighbors probably think I'm a bit crazy, because I'll "woo-hoo" at the top of my lungs with the windows open. You just can't help yourself when the inspired moment hits. In fact, just the other day, when I was taking my daughter for a walk... the air was perfect, the sky was pink and the birds were singing a beautiful song. I found myself walking down the street shouting, "You ROCK, God! You ROCK!" The moment had completely consumed me; I was deeply connected to Source.

Another way these moments express themselves are also in what I call "quiet thank you" moments. These are when the deep feeling of God's presence is nearly beyond words and it's all I can do to close my eyes and whisper, "thank you, God" often with tears of gratitude welling up in my eyes. I have these moments often when I watch my daughter sleep.

Once you've had a "woo-hoo" or a "quiet thank you" moment, you'll never forget how it feels. You can always reflect on what it was like to be filled with a sense of ease, flow, grace, trust, power and the spark of the Divine within.

It's moments like these, and you've had them too, when all is right in the world.

Now, how do you maintain that connection? The answer here is quite simple, but not necessarily easy: you seek to have those experiences more often and with more regularity. As your awareness turns toward "woo-hoo" and "quiet thank you" moments, you cant' help but experience more of them. The key here is continual conscious awareness.

Like this moment, for instance. No matter what your circumstances may be, there is something you can do right now to experience a "woo-hoo" or "quiet thank you" moment. The fact that this book made it into your hands and you're reading this right now is reason enough to be filled with a reflective "thank you." Moments like this are there for you to enjoy, as soon as you focus your attention on noticing them. Here are a few of my favorite "woo-hoo" and "thank you" moments. Let them be reminders of all the possibilities for deep connection in your own life. Maybe you'll even be inspired to enjoy a moment right now experiencing one of these moments:

- Go outside and lay in the grass under a tree.
- Read a "thank you' letter or email from a cherished client.

- Call a friend who makes you laugh.
- Prepare a cup of hot tea and write in your journal.
- Dance to your favorite song.
- Look for "shapes" in the clouds.
- Reflect on your greatest successes this year.
- Take a brisk walk.
- Cuddle with a loved one (maybe your pet).
- Pray.
- Listen to a piece of inspirational music.
- Create a vision board.
- Burn a candle and reflect on its light.
- Soak in a warm aromatherapy bath.

It is your conscious awareness and desire to notice and experience more "woo-hoo" and "quiet thank you" moments that deepens and helps you maintain your connection to Source. Now, I'll share another layer of maintaining your connection. It might not sound like fun, but it's the necessary piece to make sure you continually rise to the point of conscious connection with Source.

A Disciplined Mind

Yuck. Discipline. It's not a very warm, fuzzy word. In this context it may even sound a bit harsh because, after all, we're talking about "woo-hoo" and "quiet thank you" moments. But, discipline is part of the journey, too. And, here's what I mean.

Have you ever found yourself enjoying a fabulous day

where you're in the flow and everything's coming up roses? Then, "something happens" and you are thrown for a loop. Your feeling of well-being is shaken to the core and you need to make a critical choice about how to handle the negativity that's seeping into your formerly fabulous day. In these situations you have two options:

1. **Option A:** An undisciplined mind would allow whatever happened to pull you straight down to the bottom of the abyss of self-doubt, anger, fear, lack, loathing, etc. You pull up a chair and have yourself a big 'ol pity party. After all, you deserve some pity, "something bad" just happened.

2. **Option B:** A disciplined mind would be fully aware of the power of this moment of choice and would look down the dark abyss and say, "I'm aware that you are calling me into a dark downward spiral, but I consciously choose not to go there." Then, you'll discipline yourself to seek out a "woo-hoo" or "quiet thank you" moment. You'll listen to your "Trust in Your Divine Plan" guided mediation; take some action to draw your mind (and heart) toward a positive emotion and away from the abyss of fear.

As you can see, a disciplined mind in this case, is not something to resist or ignore. It is the very thing that will help you on a moment by moment basis to rise up and maintain a higher state of being.

Another method I want to share with you to help you maintain your conscious connection with Source is something

I call a "God's eye view."

God's Eye View

Are you familiar with the expression of a "bird's eye view?" It's when you view things from a bird's perspective; far different than that which you see standing on earth. A bird's eye view allows you to grasp the entire landscape and see the interconnectedness of things that appear separate when you view them from land.

The reason I talk about a "bird's eye view" is because this concept lead me to facilitate a process at my Conscious Business Retreat, in which the participants were invited to write about their life from a "God's eye view." Grasping a sense of your life from God's perspective is an invaluable tool for every conscious entrepreneur to embrace.

What do you think God would say about your life right now, where you've been and where you're going? Reflect for a moment and let me say that again. What do you think God would say about your life right now, where you've been and where you're going? Interesting perspective to think about, isn't it?

I doubt that thoughts of lack and limitation would even enter His mind. Because the one Source (God) is the ultimate unlimited Source of all abundance in the world, and that is exactly the perspective he would have on your life; that all things are conspiring for your highest and most divine self-expression in the world. And, that your highest good is already there for you.

So, now I invite you into the 4-step process of taking a look at your life from a God's Eye View. Let's get started.

Step 1: Reflect on Your Past

Take a moment to reflect on your past. Identify some of the peaks and valleys of your prior experience. Connect with who you've become as a result of all these experiences... the good and the not so good. Look to see how your past experiences have brought you wisdom, strength, love, insight, commitment, passion, conviction, friendship, resourcefulness, resolve, etc. Allow yourself to see the Divine Order of each and every experience and imagine what God would have said to you at each point along your journey.

Step 2: Connect with This Moment

Next, allow yourself to connect deeply with this moment, and the life that you are currently living. Embrace all of your current successes and dreams along with any challenges that may be showing up in your life right now. Allow yourself to fully appreciate the place that you're at today. And, again, allow yourself to see the Divine Order of each and every experience. And imagine what God would say to you in this moment.

Step 3: Look to Your Future

Look forward on the path that lies ahead of you. Let your imagination flourish as you envision everything your heart desires becoming real for you. Envision your life as it unfolds perfectly, even exceeding your greatest dreams. As you envision your future, leave room for things you can't imagine right now... knowing that God's plan for your life is so much bigger than that which you can see from your human perspective. And again, allow yourself to see the Divine Order of each and every future experience and imagine what God would say about the path that lies ahead.

Step 4: Write your God's Eye View
Now, in a space of quietude, perhaps outside in nature, or in front of a glowing candle, review the above three steps. Begin to write freely about your past, present and future experiences... as if you were God writing about what he sees in (and for) your life. Let your imagination and creativity soar as you envision "God's Eye View." In case you are stuck getting started, here's a line you can use to begin the process: "As God, in this elevated perspective, I can see every step of your journey as divinely guided by me. I see..."

I've recorded a guided meditation to go along with the "God's Eye View" exercise. You can download it at **www.TheFreedomFormula.com/guide**

ACTION GUIDE EXERCISE #10

Journal about your discoveries after listening to the God's Eye View meditation.

www.TheFreedomFormula.com/guide

Take some time with this exercise and write as much as you'd like. The more detail and wisdom you allow to flow through you, the more benefit this exercise will be to you, especially over time because you'll come back to read this over and over again. Every time you feel stopped, or filled with fear, lack or doubt, you can take out what you've written and remind yourself of the perfection of the divine unfolding of your life.

The Source of Your Relationships

I didn't want to complete this section on your connection to your Source, without bringing to light the value of your relationships in strengthening this connection. You may be asking what your relationships with others have to do with your connection to Source? The answer is everything.

It is through your relationships with others that you're able to experience yourself as an expression of God's love in the world. This holds true in all of your relationships, both business and personal. They are all vehicles that give you a deeper experience of yourself.

Neale Donald Walsch said it best in our interview. He talked about peace, love and harmony in the world beginning across our dinner table, across the pillow, across the front seat of the car and in the boardrooms and meeting halls of the world. In other words, we demonstrate our highest self through our relationships with others.

That being said, I simply invite you to be a source of peace, harmony and love in your relationships. With these as daily, tangible experiences, you'll constantly be calling forth more and more of your Divine expression in the world, and this in turn will bring you closer to an everyday connection with Source.

As a conscious business owner, a powerful vehicle to "call forth" your divine gifts is your relationships with your prospects, clients and customers. Sadly, I see many entrepreneurs doing great with regard to their connection to Source, but they completely miss the point when it comes to connecting with their market. Without the connection to your market, you have no business. Which means your gifts are not being shared to the degree they could be, and your business isn't experiencing the success it could be.

I have to admit this is the piece that frustrates me the most because I see it all the time. I meet business owners with incredible gifts and talents, but they're unwilling to get serious about the business of their business (marketing and money) because they say, "God will provide for me." Yes, that's absolutely true. God does provide. But, money doesn't drop from the heavens; it is given to you through human hands, directed by God, in exchange for the products and services you provide and market.

You have a divine responsibility to be a beacon for those you are meant to serve. You must be clear about who your market is and how you can reach them with your message. And, you need to embrace the monetary value of your product or service and ask for what you're worth!

This, fellow conscious entrepreneurs, is why it's time to take a look at connecting with your market.

What Business Are You In?

Many conscious entrepreneurs fail in business because they're so engrossed in "the work" they neglect doing what it takes to turn "the work" into a successful conscious business. I admit, I made this mistake for many years of my business. Then, one of my mentors made an alarm go off in my head. She said that whatever business I thought I was in, I was wrong. She said no matter what product or service I offered, that wasn't my business. I was in the business of marketing. Why? Because without marketing there is no business. My business changed on that day, because she was right. Marketing (or the lack of it) is what helps your business sink or swim.

Please take a deep breath right now. If the thought of marketing makes your stomach turn, don't worry. I'm going to shed some light on marketing from a conscious perspective and why it's so important for you to embrace. First, I want to drive home a point I made earlier about money... because marketing is the tangible tool that brings you money.

Money comes to you in exchange for your product or service that solves a problem for your clients and customers. Money does not flow to you just because you meditate for hours, have a vision board on your wall, and have a strong intention to attract clients. Don't get me wrong, all of these intangible/spiritual components are integral to your success. But, you must connect all of your intangible/inner/spiritual work with the physical/tangible/real world through conscious action! It's the integration of spirituality and business in the physical world that leads to more soul in your business, and more money in your bank! You've got to be blending BOTH worlds to really succeed.

Let's face it, nobody ever had a bag of money drop on their head while they were meditating on the mountain top. But, bags of money have dropped in the hands of entrepreneurs who maintain the vibration of meditating on the mountain top... while working in the physical plane to serve their prospects, customers and clients by helping them solve their problems.

Who Wants Your Product or Service

There's a reason why I'm so adamant about bridging the gap between your spiritual nature (which is the Source of the gifts and passions you want to share in your business) and the market you will serve. Unfortunately, many conscious entrepreneurs begin their business with a great idea... a dream. Usually, this idea or dream feels like a spark of the Divine; like you were given the idea to take action and go forth in changing the world. This is good! But, here's the mistake I see happening everywhere. In fact, it's one of the biggest mistakes I've made in the past.

You ignore doing your homework to identify WHO will BUY what you want to sell. And, every single entrepreneur on the planet is in sales, whether you like it or not. So, it's time to make friends with the reality that you will be selling your product or service. I'm not talking about the "cheesy car salesman" type of selling. I'm talking about selling something you believe in (you) because you know your product or service matches the needs of your prospect or client. It has nothing to do with "closing the deal" but everything to do with "opening a conversation" about the ways in which you solve problems for your clients.

Many wannabe business owners fall into the trap of not getting clear about who their market is, if there's a demand for their product or service, and the reality that they'll need to market and sell their products or services. They believe the idea they were given was a gift from God and MUST be destined to work in the marketplace, or you wouldn't have been given the idea in the first place.

Here's a glimpse of how this occurs in my own life. I receive a Divine spark in the form of a business idea, and immediately I take it to the highest, best possible outcome. In my mind, I easily make millions of dollars, and create spreadsheets to calculate projected income. If I sold x amount of widgets at x amount per sale, I'd yield x amount of dollars. And, I do that line after line for all the different income streams that are possible from this one idea. Yes, I guess you could say I go a bit overboard with it.

But here's the important part. I enjoy exploring the idea and the fantasy, but take action on very few of the ideas. You see, ideas are literally a dime a dozen. It's the ideas that are divinely sparked AND match an already existing demand in the marketplace that you find the idea that is one in a million. Rhonda Bhyrne's movie, *The Secret,* is a great example of a Divine idea matched with an eager market. So, allow the ideas to flow to and through you, and enjoy the fantasy of several multi-million dollar businesses, but be very careful as to which ideas you pursue in the real world. You will waste time, money and energy pursuing a great idea that doesn't match a market demand.

Let me rephrase that. The money, time and energy will not be wasted, because each action you take will teach you valuable lessons, give you new insight, and point you further down the path of your destiny. So, no matter how challenging an endeavor might be, you will have never wasted time because you and your business will have evolved from the experience.

Here's something interesting to note about marketing and sales and relating it to your business. The alignment of your product or service and the marketplace may not be apparent at first glimpse. The connection may not be blatantly obvious. This is when you can get creative about how your business evolves and how you position yourself to match a need in the market. Your product or service always remains true to who you are; but how you evolve, promote, position and market yourself, the words you write on your brochure and website, the way you package your products and services and communicate your brand position can be angled to create a match where it wasn't previously obvious.

Let me share an example of this in my own life to illustrate what I'm talking about here. In my prior business, I owned a yoga studio in Los Angeles. This business came forth from my personal passion for yoga as a fitness regimen and as a vehicle to more deeply explore my spiritual nature. I loved yoga so much; I became a trained and certified teacher and started my yoga business. I knew, first hand, the impact yoga had on people's lives, far beyond the physical realm.

There was something magical about creating and holding a space for others to have an experience of their radiant, divine self through yoga. This is what kept my business plugging along year after year... creating space for others to experience their magic. I ended up teaching high-end clients ranging from celebrities like Reba McEntire to retired 45-year old multi-millionaire philanthropists. Even though these clients paid me well and were very rewarding to work with, I didn't have enough of them to support my business.

So, while I enjoyed success in terms of a sense of fulfillment and purpose, financially my yoga business wasn't making it. This was the business that nearly drove me into bankruptcy. I was paying a high-end rent in one of the "hottest" neighborhoods in Los Angeles and had a staff of a dozen instructors. There were weeks that I personally taught nearly thirty classes to help make ends meet. But, they never did, my expenses were simply too high for the business to ever make sense. (A perfect illustration of why it's important to do your due diligence and research first to make sure an idea will actually work! Please learn from my experience.)

The day I sold my studio (for next to nothing) I walked out the door for the last time with a huge sense of relief and a sense of loss. I would miss the magic that had been shared within those studio walls. I would miss the gift of creating the space for my students to experience and know their greatness. Some of my deepest moments of feeling connected to Source, were when I sat at the end of a class feeling the profound stillness and Presence in the room after I had guided my students into savasana (final relaxation).

It'll be no surprise to find out that my favorite part of the meetings for the Network for Empowering Women Entrepreneurs was at the end of the meetings when I would lead a powerful guided meditation as all of the women held hands and stood in a large circle around the room. Again, I was elated by the experience of creating a sacred space for the members to experience their greatness. But, as you know, this business wasn't built on a foundation for success either.

However, I began to recognize the theme of "creating space for others to experience their greatness." No matter what I did, this was always at the heart of my passion and had been for years. The problem here was that there wasn't a viable market for a business whose purpose was "to hold space for possibility." Nobody was looking that up in the yellow pages or running a Google search to pay someone to "hold space."

Thankfully, by now I had learned enough about business and marketing that I started thinking and planning from a strategic perspective, which I had never done before. I was smart enough to realize a "holding space" business would never make it. Rather, I began doing my own personal inquiry and a lot of outside research to see how this passion could translate to meeting the needs of a market that already existed, and would pay me well. I was ready to finally build a successful business that made a lot of money.

As a result of this new awareness and my personal and business evolution, I introduced a new business and finally found my "sweet spot." My new business, Love Your Life, LLC, offers conscious business coaching and book publishing for inspired entrepreneurs. This business integrated my passion for "creating and holding space for others" with very tangible business strategies and tactics that work in the real world. With this business I feel like I found my piece of heaven on earth. It meets the four components of a conscious business (make money, make a difference, be who you are, trust in your Divine Plan) and sometimes I feel like I should be paying my clients because I experience such joy in working with them. Everything I've experienced, every new marketing strategy I've learned, every success or challenge I'd had up to this point, made SENSE in my new business. It all came together because I dared to investigate how my passion could be shared with an already existing market using a business model that worked.

This is what I invite you to look for in your business. Look for the theme of what truly sings to you (for me it was "holding space for others"). Then, get creative about how you can do your work for a market that will pay you. For me, the entrepreneurial market was a natural fit. Entrepreneurs are on a mission to experience their greatness and to use their business as a vehicle for their highest self-expression. They are truly my perfect clients. And, they're a market that, generally speaking, is willing to pay for products and services that bring them closer to their goals and dreams; whether it is through coaching or helping them get their book done.

To illustrate this point of connecting your "work" to a market demand that already exists, I'll take my story one step further. It was through my women's organization that I had established my small independent publishing company to help my members become published authors in a series of inspirational anthologies for women. For three years I had viewed my publishing company as a completely separate entity; I had seen it as a commodity based business focused on delivering a specific good... a book; like most publishers out there. It was about the book, not necessarily about the author's evolution. Until, I embarked on my journey of bringing together my passions and my experience into one unified, highly market-able business.

What I discovered was my endeavor into book publishing was an avenue for me to "create and hold space for entrepre-neurial authors." And the market is huge! Having a book is one of the most powerful marketing tools for any business owner, especially a conscious business owner who sees having a book as the integration of the soul of the business (the message in the book) and the "business" of business (the marketing). Plus, there is a market driven need for ethical, reliable, book publishing resources that understand the needs of entrepreneurs.

Writing a book is like birthing a baby. It is a deeply spiri-tual experience (even for my clients who don't consider them-selves "spiritual"). Authors often feel exposed and vulnerable and have doubts and fears that come up about putting their heart and soul onto the pages of a book for everyone to see. The most important role I play for my authors is to hold the space of what's possible for them through the process of writing, promoting and marketing their book. And, it's been a miracle to see the shifts that occur as my clients step further into their journey of writing and revealing the soul of their business through their books. Their energy, confidence, clarity and focus dramatically increase and as a result, they experience greater success even before the book is done.

My passion for "holding space for others" that began back in my yoga studio carries through everything I do now. But, now this passion is packaged, promoted and marketed in a way that naturally attracts my ideal clients. So, this is what I encourage you to begin to do for your own business. Look for the themes, look for your passions and open yourself up to discovering other ways to creatively package and present your work so it matches the need of a market that will pay you.

My business wouldn't be successful if my headlining benefit was "holding space." Nobody would pay me for that. But, when it's packaged and presented in a way that meets an existing market need, the money easily flows in exchange for the products and services I offer.

You can find out more about Love Your Life, LLC at **www.LoveYourLife.com**

OK, I realize this was a somewhat lengthy illustration, but after reading my story, I trust you'll now realize how important it is to not just jump at any idea that crosses your mind (like I did with my yoga studio and women's organization). You'll see its worth taking the time to strategize, position and research your business concept before you invest thousands of dollars on hiring a graphic designer, building a website, and developing a new product or service. You're in for a long uphill climb if you don't create a business that fulfills an existing need.

Now, you may be saying that you can educate your prospects to realize they do have a need. Then, once you've convinced them of a particular need, pain or want, then you can introduce your product or service as the solution. And yes, you can take this approach. But, it takes a lot longer to see results.

I want you to find what many marketers call the low hanging fruit. The low hanging fruit are considered to be those prospects that already have a need and are a looking for a solution to their problem or challenge. They are referred to as low hanging fruit because all you need to do is find them and easily pick them from the tree. I know that's not the best visual in town, but if you've ever been to an apple orchard to pick apples, you know that it's much easier to get the low hanging fruit because they are ripe and ready to be picked.

If you offer a product or service that doesn't have an already existing need, it's like going to the apple orchard and having to find a ladder to climb your way up to the fruit and then balance on your tip toes to use a pole to get the fruit down. Now, why would you do that when you can walk up to the tree, leave the ladder at home, and pluck off an apple at shoulder height? Enough about apples, let's get back to your prospective market. Just remember the concept of looking for the low hanging fruit.

Determine If There's a Market

There are several different ways you can determine if there is a market for your product or service. It can be as simple as a Google search to see if other people have successful businesses in an area similar to that which you want to pursue. I also recommend you go to the bookstore and look on the shelves to see if there are books on the topic you want to create your business around.

The more research you do, and the more similar enterprises you find, the better. Let me say that again. The more research you do, and the MORE similar enterprises you find, the better. The reason why it's great to see other businesses succeed in the area you want to (or are) pursuing is because their success proves to you that there is a market demand for the product or service. Plus, if you find a company that is already enjoying a certain level of success in the field you are interested in pursuing, you can learn from them and have their company serve as a model. Modeling is done all the time in business. Business owners learn from their peers to see what's working and not working in the marketplace. It's completely ethical to model another business, as long as you don't copy exactly what they're doing. You still need to make it your own. But, at least some of the homework and research is already done for you… by them.

Narrow Your Market

So, once you've identified there is a viable market for your new idea or dream, or you've evolved your idea to the point where you know there's a market match (like I did) you need to further identify who your target market is. Listen up here. Your target market isn't who you THINK you can get as a client; it's who you WANT to get as a client. You need to become crystal clear on who your target market is, because this will help you execute a marketing plan that simultaneously attracts those people you feel called to work with, and repels those people you don't. Repel may be a strong word, but it's true. Your Divine gift is not going to be expressed at its highest potential when you have clients who drain your energy, don't pay you enough money, make mountains out of mole hills and don't respect your time. And, that's exactly what happens when you attract the wrong type of client.

I trust you're beginning to grasp the importance of doing your research first. You may be kicking and screaming that you just want to go for the dream, but take it from one who has done it that way in the past; it's so much better to do the research early on so you can build a business on a solid foundation for long-lasting, joyous success.

ACTION GUIDE EXERCISE #11

Who is your target market? And, how do you know this market is viable?

www.TheFreedomFormula.com/guide

Take Research One Step Further

Once you've identified who your target market is, you can then take your research one step further by surveying those people you've identified as your best potential customers. One method of surveying your target market is simply to create a list of questions and call your prospects (assuming you already have a relationship with them) to request a few minutes of their time. Then, let them know you value their opinion and that you'd like them to help you with your market research by answering a few questions. It helps to give them a small gift in exchange for answering the survey (i.e. a 15-minute consultation, a free-report, downloadable audio, etc.)

The questions you ask should be crafted to provide information about your target market's specific problems and challenges. Having them tell you specifically what challenges they face is invaluable information for you to use in your marketing and promotions. It allows you to learn the language that your target market uses to describe their needs. Remember, the words are how you communicate and connect with your market, so they need to resonate with your market in order to get them to act.

One final thing you'll want to do on this survey call is to introduce your product or service idea and ask for their feedback on what components they'd like to see added or tweaked in order for it to really solve their problem. If you can get your target client to outline what it would take for them to do business with you, you've got some fantastic concepts to implement into your business to make it a "no-brainer" to your market.

If you have a large group of people you want to survey, the phone call method may not be the most effective. In this case you may prefer using an online survey database. This is where you create a survey online to ask your questions. Then, you simply send the link to your target people and ask them to click to your survey and answer the questions. Here are a few resources you can check out online: www.SurveyMonkey.com   www.AskDatabase.com   and www.FreedBack.com

The incentive for doing this type of research about your idea is that when you've made a match, and your ideal client finds you and pays you for services you love to give, it often feels like a joyful, synchronistic Divine intervention. And, it can be added to the list of "woo-hoo" moments. You'll feel grateful and blessed to have attracted them and they'll feel grateful and blessed to have found you. There is an energy that occurs between the two of you that flows magnificently when you are doing work you love, with a client you love, and who loves and appreciates you. It's one big Divine love fest.

But, it takes some serious marketing focus and business strategy to pave the way for these Divine connections to occur. Your job is to lay down the path by gaining clarity, matching your passion to a marketing need and putting a solid foundation under your business. Once that's done, you can focus more freely on maintaining your light, maintaining your high vibration, and staying connected with your Source. From there, the Universe receives your clear signal that you are truly ready to enjoy a purpose-driven business and a soul-satisfying life.

The secret to your success is in your ability to integrate both of these aspects of your business: your spiritual nature and evolution, as well as your business savvy and marketing smarts. This is where you'll discover the sweet spot in your business.

Design Your Business

(Soul + Connection + Design + I) x E = F

Now that you've discovered the soul of your business and learned about connecting to Source and to your market, you're ready for the process of designing your business, and your life. I use the word design, rather than plan, because this is the step where you look at the big, broad vision for your business and your life. This is the part where you get to think big, dream your dreams, envision your highest Divine expression and design the life and the business you want. This step will align you more with the spiritual aspects of your business, whereas implementation (which we'll cover next) pertains more to the specific actions you'll begin taking to have the "rubber hit the road" in the real world.

'How' Is None Of Your Business

This is one of my favorite statements. I first heard it at a workshop at the Agape Spiritual Center in Culver City, California and it's been a mantra of mine ever since. It's a phrase that comes in very handy in this third step. Because when you first begin to design your business, you may be tempted to limit your vision to that which you see as logical and possible from where you stand today. You'll limit yourself to include only those things you know how to do; those things that feel somewhat safe and real.

But, for the purpose of this step, I encourage you to ignore "reality" and allow yourself to stretch beyond the limits of your rational, planning, logical mind. Instead, you'll embrace everything you've learned in this book so far about the soul of your business (you) and your connection to Source and your market, and from there you'll elevate yourself to your God's eye view, and the infinite abundant supply of the Universe. This is the space in which you'll design your business and your life.

Place Your Order

This concept was made quite popular in the hit movie "The Secret." All you need to do is place your order with the Universe and it will begin aligning in such a way that your order is received, as long as your energy is a match to the vibration of that which you desire. Much like you don't question getting your eggs over easy when you go out for breakfast. You place your order, expect the eggs to be delivered to your table and what d'ya know? They show up just as you had ordered. So, this is the energy in which you'll begin designing your business, by placing your order with the Universe.

But, let me add one cautionary note here before proceeding. While it's important to expand your vision, to go beyond that which you know how to do from where you stand today, it's also important that you don't create a vision that makes you say to yourself, "You're crazy. That's impossible. Who do you think you are? That'll never happen." Because that which you think about, you bring about, and your dream will never be realized.

The vision for your business and your life must be a stretch for you, and out of your current comfort zone, but not so far out that you have a negative association with it. If every time you focus on your vision you instantly connect with feelings of fear, lack or doubt, you're doing yourself a disservice. The life you design for yourself should be one that brings forth feelings of excitement, enthusiasm and ecstatic joy. Not doubt and fear. Remember, you don't have to know how to accomplish the dream. You simply need to be clear about what it is, believe the vision, and keep yourself away from fear, doubt and lack.

Your emotional state is a huge factor in living the business (and life) you desire. So, it's important for you to continually experience joy, love, happiness, nurturing, compassion, etc. and stay in the higher, better feeling emotions. Use this as a caution to make sure your big vision makes you feel good, rather than bad.

Speed Matters

You may be asking how to walk this fine line between creating an expansive vision, and not having it bring up negative emotions. I want to share a principle here that will help you walk this line with ease, trust and joy. This is something I learned walking through my own challenges along the entrepreneurial journey. Because, let's face it, it's not easy to create a whole new and exciting vision for your business (and your life) when you don't know where your next month's rent (or sometimes your next day's meal) is coming from.

The principle is that of speed. Often, when you think of speed, you think of executing an action in the physical world. The speed in which you make a follow-up call, gather information, get a product to market, make more money, build your website, etc. It's all about the physical, tangible world of "making things happen."

But, the speed I'm talking about here, to keep you energized and inspired about your vision, is the speed in which you reconnect to your Source when the feelings of fear, doubt, despair or lack creep in. When you're able to raise your awareness to the infinite supply of the Universe and to the Divine Perfection of your life, you'll see that whatever is happening in the moment is part of the Divine Plan. You'll be able to manage the negative emotions more easily and rise back up into the higher emotional states much more quickly.

No matter how difficult a challenge you may be facing, the ability to connect with Source quickly is the key to moving through it. This principle really showed itself to me when I experienced a miscarriage with my second baby. I had wanted nothing more than to bring another child into our family. You can imagine my despair when I miscarried the day after Christmas in 2006 (after having announced the pregnancy as a gift to our families on Christmas day). I remember when the loss finally hit me on a deep emotional level four days later; I simply crumbled into a pile of tears on the cold tile floor in my bathroom. I sobbed uncontrollably at the depth of the loss I experienced in miscarrying.

But, during my intense and cathartic cry, I somehow made my way to my journal and began to write about what I was experiencing. Through my writing, I was able to reconnect with Source and the feeling that somehow, this too, was happening in alignment with my Divine Plan. I shifted how I related to my loss and despair and gained a new perspective in which to move through this experience… right in the middle of the moment I was feeling it the deepest. The speed in which I consciously connected to Source was integral in the rapid and radical transformations I made in my life and my business as a result of this loss in my life.

I trust you're beginning to see how it is possible to create a vision larger than anything you've dreamed of before, while managing any negative emotions that come along with that vision. You maintain a conscious awareness of the infinite abundance of the Universe/God.

In the world of high performance sports training they do something called speed drills, where the sole focus of the exercise is to consistently increase speed. Consider this your own personal speed drill. It may take a while to strengthen your speed "muscles" because they may have become atrophied over time. Right now you get to recondition those "muscles" to respond to heavier and heavier loads. The "load" in this case is the size of your vision, and the negative emotions that may surface when you're scared of it. The more expansive your vision is, the heavier the load is; which means you have more resistance to work with. The beauty of this is that it's an opportunity to delve into your spirituality and connect with Source more deeply than ever before.

Now that you've set the stage in your mind and heart for managing the emotions that may come along with your vision, you're ready to begin designing your business, and your life. The world is an abundant Source, and you can have everything you desire. So, enjoy this process and allow your joy, excitement and enthusiasm to shine through.

Step 1: Identifying Your Values

The first step in designing your business (and your life) is to identify your values. This is the foundation on which everything will grow. The reason your values are so important is because your values support you in experiencing long-term sustainable success, as well as keeping you from compromising yourself for the sake of your dreams. If you design your business with disregard for your values, you're setting yourself up for a long, challenging road that won't be any fun. There is no dream unless it allows you to experience your values each and every day.

BusinessDictionary.com shares this definition of values:

Values: *In general: Important and enduring beliefs or ideals shared by the members of a culture about what is good or desirable and what is not. Values exert major influence on the behavior of an individual and serve as broad guidelines in all situations.*

For example, one of my values is family which, for me, includes being a good mom and caring wife. Considering that my husband is a stay-at-home-Dad (the best one on the planet), it would be easy for me to work from 8 AM to 10PM and know that my daughter is in the loving care of my husband. But, that wouldn't honor my value of family. So, I make it a point to cook dinner at least three times a week, attend a weekly mom's group with my daughter, take family walks around the neighborhood, sit down for dinner together every night (with rare exception if I'm out of town) and take Friday's off to give my husband a day to himself while I enjoy being with my daughter. Oh, and I rarely work after 5:00 PM and don't work on Fridays or on weekends, unless there's an extreme circumstance.

Another little trick for me to connect with my value of family is to bake pies. I never made a pie in my life until I met my husband; he's got a real hankering for pie, so I made it a hobby to learn how to make them. Lucky for me, I discovered that it really is 'easy as pie.' There's something about baking a pie that nurtures my husband, our family and my self. Baking a pie instantly makes me feel like a wife and mother. And, quite honestly, sometimes I forget that part of myself when I'm in my office diligently working on a project.

The thing to remember about designing a business (and a life) that supports your values is that you'll be working at a different pace than many other entrepreneurs who sacrifice their values for the sake of their business. This is not what conscious business is about. So, be prepared to move a bit slower than your colleagues who work eighty hours a week.

And, know that you are on a journey and all is happening in Divine right time. You don't need to keep up with anyone. This is all about what works for YOU!

So, now I invite you to reflect on your own values. Don't worry if you discover you're not living your life according to these right now, that's OK. Simply notice (without judging yourself) if there is disparity between your values, and your current life, and become aware of those things you'd like to experience differently than you are now. Your values are there as guideposts to anchor you in your belief of what's important... while you work toward realizing your dreams for your business, and your life.

ACTION GUIDE EXERCISE #12

This exercise invites you to identify your core values.

www.TheFreedomFormula.com/guide

To help you get started, here's a list of some common values I see in my clients. Which of these resonate with you?

Accomplishment   Family
Adventure   Freedom
Beauty   Friendship
Community   Fun
Creativity   Gratitude

Health	Prosperity
Honesty	Respect
Leadership	Self-Care
Learning	Spirituality
Meaning	Success
Money	Trust
Personal Growth	Wisdom

When you live your life as a reflection of your values, and take actions to LIVE your values, your ability to manifest increases greatly. Because when your values are reflected throughout your life, you have more energy and enthusiasm for all that you do and this increased energy and enthusiasm becomes a magnet for you to attract more of what you desire, which leads to more energy and more enthusiasm. Living your life as a demonstration of your values becomes the base of a continual upward spiral toward your highest and best good.

Step 2: Focusing on Your Priorities

Now that you've identified your values, the next step in designing your business is to identify your priorities. Your priorities will help you make decisions about your business and your life to determine what takes precedence. Entrepreneurs have a tendency to think that everything is equally important and/or urgent. But, this is the very thinking that keeps entrepreneurs stagnant and not making measurable progress in any area. Being spread too thin because everything is "important" is a sure-fire road to burnout, frustration and financial strain. To succeed as a conscious entrepreneur you need to identify your highest priorities and let them guide you when you feel yourself being pulled off track.

For the sake of this exercise, I'd like you only to identify your top five priorities. If your list gets longer than that it can become overwhelming. Narrowing it down to your top five makes it short, simple and powerful.

Your priorities are based on your values but taken one step further. You create your priorities in a hierarchical order with those higher up on the list being the most important. The reason you rank them in order is so you can use them to help you make important decisions in your business and your life. For example, let's say your highest priority is your health; you can use this as a motivator to wake up just a little bit earlier to get your workout in before the day starts. The interesting thing about this is if you consistently say you're going to get up early to exercise and don't, then health may not be your top priority, even though you say you want it to be. If they're truly your priorities, they'll cause you to make a change in your life.

When you are fully committed to living by your priorities, (and not only wishful thinking), you're telling the Universe you're serious about living the life you say you want. Your priority-based actions in the physical world act like rocket-fuel for your dreams to be realized.

So, use your priorities as a way to show the Universe you are committed to living your best life, so you can be the highest and fullest expression of your self. It's when you live in this place of full self-expression that your Divine gifts shine and your contribution to the world is magnified exponentially. So, if you've ever thought of priorities as something that "isn't for you," it's time to rethink your relationship to them. Because, when all is said and done, living by your priorities is a way to experience more of your Divine self!

Now, I don't know about you, but when I learned about priorities in terms of my business, nobody ever told me they were a way for me to connect with my Divine self. But, that's what they are. Just like your values, they serve as your guide-posts to help you be fully who you are, and attract that which you desire.

Now that you have an understanding of the importance of your priorities, it's time for you to identify yours.

ACTION GUIDE EXERCISE #13

This exercise invites you to identify your top 5 priorities, based on your values.

www.TheFreedomFormula.com/guide

Go ahead and review your values list and from that, write down your top five priorities. Once you've written your five priorities, take some time to review them and see if they are in the right order for you. If the order of priorities shifts after some reflection, shift the order on your list to reflect what is true for you.

This list of priorities, in order of importance, is an important tool in keeping you focused and on track. If one day you're bombarded with distractions and are pulled off track, you can refer back to this list to regain your focus and to bring peace to your decision making process. During a hectic day I've said to myself, "There are so many things to do, I don't know where to start." No more! I just refer to this list and the answer is simple: start with the priorities. And, now you can, too.

Step 3: Creating Your Lifestyle Vision

Your lifestyle vision is one that includes everything about your life. Too often, when you get into traditional business visioning, this element is completely left out of the equation. But, for the conscious entrepreneur this is where it has to begin. Your life is your business; it is a Divine expression of you. There is no separation between you, your life and your business. As in everything in life, you are all one. There is only one life being expressed through you, not bits and pieces of lives expressed in different areas of your life.

It's the integration of the whole that you're creating here. I think this is why so many corporate employees decide to start their own business; they became tired of having to compartmentalize the whole of their life for the sake of the part that was climbing higher up the corporate ladder. The view from the top of the ladder is dismal: when you don't see your family or friends, you have no connection to your spiritual self and your health is on the skids.

The concept of integration isn't new, it's been around for ages, but it's finally coming to the forefront as our culture realizes that there is so much more to success than the acquisition of money. Money, in and of itself, is un-gratifying. It's a piece of paper with numbers on it. But, when money is used to help you express more and more of who you Divinely are in the world, then money is serving its purpose; for you to be more of who you are, for your gifts to shine more brightly in the world and for you to make a larger positive impact on the people whose lives you touch. That is what money is for. And, this is why I wrote this book; for the ever growing population of entrepreneurs who want to create a successful business and live their life according to their highest aspirations for a fully integrated, fully expressed and financially abundant life.

Your vision can include the generalities of your business (because that is an integral part of your life) but leave the detailed vision for your business to the next step. For now, simply focus on your vision for your whole life. This vision, when complete, should evoke positive emotions and increase your energy and enthusiasm for your life!

On the following page I've listed several areas that you'll want to consider when creating your big vision. As you write about all of these areas, include the details of each one and especially how you feel about that particular area in your dream life. Keep in mind as you proceed, how you will experience yourself through the manifestation of living this vision.

To help you get started, here are some areas to consider when writing your lifestyle vision:

Home

Family

Friends

Geographic location

Emotional state of being

Expressions of love

Travel

Spirituality

Daily ritual

Environment

Recreation

Fitness

Social Involvement

Giving Back/Philanthropy

Personal development

Business growth

Financial goals

Emotional well-being

ACTION GUIDE EXERCISE #14

Write the vision for your life/lifestyle.

www.TheFreedomFormula.com/guide

If you'd like to take this exercise one step further, create a vision board specifically to be a physical representation of your written lifestyle vision. Then, hang your vision board on a wall in your home or office and reflect on it regularly. While you take time to reflect, do so with a feeling of positive energy coursing through your being as if everything on your vision board were real in your life today.

Let God Into Your Vision

As you create your vision, keep in mind the element of the unknown and allow God into your vision. What I mean by this is even though your vision may feel big, huge, exciting and awesome to you, still, God sees so much more. It's impossible to know just what miracles and gifts are in store for you. So, to make room for (and invite) the unknown, write this statement at the end of your vision: This or Something Better! This statement is like hanging a sign for God that says, "I'm open to receive that which you see for me, even bigger and better than I can see for myself. Thank you in advance for the gifts you'll bestow on me."

Step 4: Creating Your Business Vision

Your business vision is created within the context of your lifestyle vision. Your lifestyle vision is about the whole of your life, and, your business vision is specific to your business.

The more clarity you have about your business vision, the more energy you have to consciously create and attract everything you desire for this vision to be realized. Until you experience the power of clarity, it's like a ship sailing through the night with no idea where it is, or where it's going, and without a navigation system. As soon as the ship knows its latitude and longitude, and where it's going, the navigation system directs it right to port. The same goes for your business. Clarity is power!

I know from personal experience the cost of not being clear about my business. In fact, I struggled for years when I went to networking meetings (or anywhere) and people asked me what I did. I'd often stumble on my words, say something different every time I answered the question and whatever I said landed like a "flat-line" on the other person's ears. It's a horrible feeling. I believe part of this came from trying to fit in with everyone else and model that which I'd seen as successful, but not quite right for me. This is why the first step of *The Freedom Formula* is about discovering the soul of YOUR business. Clarity on this helps you gain clarity on everything.

As you develop your business vision, do your best to describe in detail what you do, how you do it, how you feel when doing it, how others help you, how your clients' lives change, how you impact the world around you, etc. Just like in your lifestyle vision, this is all written with the belief the Universe may have something bigger and better in store for you. So, don't hesitate to be specific, to include numbers, to anticipate gross revenues, bottom-line profit, expansion plans or anything else that feels concrete. Just know that you're not limited to the scope of your own imagination, only to the scope of God's imagination. Thus, it's important to include at the end of your business vision, the words: This Or Something Better.

Take as much time and write as many words as necessary to paint a clear picture of the business you are creating, ensuring that this vision evokes a feeling of enthusiasm and excitement within you. These positive emotions need to be associated with the vision for it to have power. As with your lifestyle vision, if you experience fear, lack or doubt as you create your dream business, take a break to reconnect with Source energy and elevate your vibration.

Once you realize you're not creating your vision alone, it gets easier to resonate with it. If it still feels scary, then shift the vision a bit so you experience positive emotions when you reflect upon it.

To help you get started with the vision for your business, here are a few things to consider:

Products and Services You Offer
Scalability
Product Funnel
Your Network
Support Team
Home-based or Bricks and Mortar
What You Do vs. What Your Team Does
Number of Hours You Work
Number of Clients
Sales Process
Customer Service
Branding
Speaking
Publicity
Visibility
Marketing
Internet Presence
Business Development

Your business vision is a way of seeing your true self through your business. When you are clear about what it is you want for your business, and what you provide for your clients and customers, success comes much more easily. Why? Because clarity is power. The more crystal clear you are about your vision, the more you can focus your energy on experiencing your vision, the more you'll connect with the clients and customers you're meant to serve and the more energy you'll have in pursuing your vision. Your vision begins a positive upwards spiral that continually draws you forward on your entrepreneurial journey.

So, take some time right now to write your vision for your business.

ACTION GUIDE EXERCISE #15

Write your vision for your business.

www.TheFreedomFormula.com/guide

Find a Vision Partner

Now that your vision is written, let's add more energy to it. As I mentioned earlier, you can create a vision board specific to your business and reflect on it regularly. Another tool I use is a visioning partner. All you need is another conscious entrepreneur who you know, like, and trust.

Once you've found a visioning partner, make an appointment to talk on the phone for fifteen minutes every week. When it's time for your call, you may want to do a brief centering exercise that aligns you with each other and establishes the sacred space in which you'll share together. Just taking a few deep breaths together can easily get you centered. (That's the yoga instructor in me speaking.) Then, simply speak your vision to your partner. As you do, their job is to listen to you, hold the vision for you, and see it as absolutely already done and coming to you now. Then, you switch roles and you listen to your visioning partner share his/her vision and hold the space for them of seeing it already done.

When working with your vision partner, you have the option to read your vision exactly as you wrote it in this exercise, or you can close your eyes, take a few deep breaths, connect to Source and speak spontaneously, in the moment, about the vision for your business, and your life. The experience of having another person listen to you with the intention of your vision being realized is deeply powerful. It's been one of the best tools I've ever used in manifesting all that has come to me in recent years from the birth of my daughter and the purchase of a brand-new custom home, to the release of one business and the rapid expansion of another. I urge you to find a partner and get started with this today because it's not only fun, it works!

CHAPTER FOUR

Implement Your Business Vision

(Soul + Connection + Design + Implementation) x E = F

Ahhh, so now it's time to bring the first three steps of *The Freedom Formula* into the physical realm with a concrete written plan you'll implement. This step is where you bring the intangible/invisible/universal principles into reality through your action. For some conscious entrepreneurs, this is a difficult step because you'd rather create, meditate, play with friends or read an inspiring book than plan. For others, this is your favorite part. Whatever previous notion you have about business planning, set it aside for now and allow this process to help you bring shape and tangible form to your visions. This is what makes implementation easy.

In my previous businesses, I found planning to be a challenge. I operated my business for years without a written plan. I kept working on project after project, and spent time working "in" my business, instead of "on" my business. Perhaps like you, I wasn't going to a bank for financing, wasn't seeking venture capital and just didn't see the point in writing one of those formal business plans that bankers and venture capitalists wanted. Those types of plans didn't feel right to me. I wanted a plan that wasn't just words on paper that someone else needed to see, but rather a guide to point me in the right direction in case I got off course.... and ensure I took aligned action to realize my vision.

I used to be a proponent of "winging it," but not so much anymore. Winging it comes in handy if you tend to procrastinate or feel stopped by fear that you're not prepared enough. Winging it causes you to take actions toward your goals before you feel prepared. There are two sides of the coin to balance here. In winging it you don't want to naively go forward with a plan that has no viable market (see chapter 2), nor do you want to get so wrapped up in the short-term project in front of you that you forget how it fits into the whole of your business. That's what happened to me; I would experience success with one project or another but I didn't have a larger view of how each project worked in relation to the overall business. I was continually starting from scratch on every project because I didn't know where I was going. And, let me tell you, that type of unplanned work takes a ton of energy. It's like having to "lift off" over and over again. Which is why I now love having a written business plan; each piece of my business makes sense now and my projects, products and services are all related to and supportive of the others.

Research shows that writing something down increases the likelihood of it being realized. Most of the motivational speakers out there talk about this specifically in relation to goals. They tell you to write down your goals in order to make them happen. And, I agree, but take it one step further. And that is to write down your plan so all of it can happen. This or something better.

What I discovered when I began talking with many of my colleagues is they didn't have a plan either. So, we decided to buddy up and work on a plan while holding each other accountable for implementing it. I'll share with you the resource we used to guide us through the process. We used the book, *One Page Business Plan* written by Jim Horan. The planning process was surprisingly easy when we followed his guidelines step by step. If you don't have the book yet, I encourage you to pick it up.

Another type of planning tool I use is my very own Sticky Note Business Plan. I knew I struck a chord with this planning method by the response I got to an article I wrote for my Email newsletter, the *Conscious Business Connection*. Here are some guidelines for creating your Sticky Note Business Plan.

Sticky Note Business Plan

My "sticky note business plan" is a simple and fun tool you can use anytime, any place to keep your business pointing in the right direction.

Here are the steps to get started birthing your plan:

1. Gather Your Planning Supplies

Thankfully, you won't need fancy computer software, or heavy reference books to write your plan. All you'll need is a wall, six poster boards, three pads of sticky notes, scotch tape, a note pad, a Sharpie marker and a pen. It'll also help to have a quiet place and a few hours of time to enjoy this process. You may even want to light your favorite candle and play some relaxing music, or invite a colleague to join you for a planning day.

2. Lay Out Your Plan

Tape the six poster boards up on the wall. Once the boards are up on the wall, grab your notepad. Sit down for a few minutes and quietly think about the aspects of your business you want to plan. For example: do you need to design a new product, produce an event, do you want to create a marketing plan or launch a new website? Do you need a timeline for the next 3 years of your business or only the next year? Is it time to introduce a new service?

Use your notepad to collect all of your ideas and decide which of the main ideas you want to use as the six categories in your plan. Next, write each category on six separate sticky notes using your Sharpie marker. Then, stick one note on the top center of each poster board… so each board is labeled for one of your six topics.

3. Download Your Ideas

Here comes the fun part. Get your pen and sticky notes and begin to write down every single idea or task that comes to mind for each category. Don't edit or censor any ideas. Simply write them down and stick them on the poster board for that category. Try to stay with one category at a time as best you can. But, if other ideas keep coming to mind, write them down and pop them on the appropriate poster. Let the ideas flow and enjoy the process of getting everything on paper.

4. Organize Your Ideas

So, now that your ideas are on the poster boards, begin to organize them. Look for themes, sequences, and categories of items. Physically move the sticky notes on the poster board to group ideas together. Sometimes I'll organize ideas by timeline, sometimes I'll organize by concept… you can organize them in the way that makes sense to you.

5. Put It All Together

Now, step back and take a look at your whole plan. After going through this process, you may discover that some items need to move higher on your priority list; while other ideas may need to be dropped from your plan completely. The right things to do (and the order in which to do them) will surface now that you have the whole plan in place. Next, rearrange the posters so the highest priority plan is at the left side of the wall and the lower priority plan is to the right side of the wall. Finally, transfer your highest priority tasks to your calendar to make sure you begin executing your plan.

6. Keep Going

As you make progress with your plan, continually re-evaluate where you are and keep moving forward with your projects. And, if you feel called to do so, once you've completed a project and your poster board is empty, you can add a new project to "the wall."

Personally, once I complete a task from one of my poster boards, I remove the sticky notes related to that task so I can visually see the space open up as I make progress with my plan. You may enjoy doing the same thing.

Now that you know how to write your "sticky note business plan," you'll discover it's actually FUN to work on your plan. And, it's a huge asset to your business, because it's easy to implement.

Time Frame

I encourage you to keep the timeline for your "sticky note business plan" to one to two years. Your business will evolve a lot in the next few years, as will you. Trying to write a detailed plan for more than two years out can be quite an undertaking. Your overall lifestyle and business vision adequately communicate the long-term vision for your business and your life. So, it's really not necessary here.

Guess what I'm going to tell you to write at the end of each poster board sticky note plan? You guessed it: This Or Something Better. As with everything in conscious business, the Divine element needs to be included, or you've missed the point. This is about planning for what you can see for yourself and your business, while remaining completely open to receiving something bigger and better from the Universe.

The plan moves you forward exponentially because with each step you implement the more you are telling the Universe you're serious about this, and you're willing to do what it takes in the physical realm to achieve your goals. Your plan is like a fluid, ever-evolving dance between the spiritual and the practical that unfolds more beautifully with each and every twist, turn and step.

A Heads Up

Let me give you a "heads up" here for a moment. As you implement more in the physical realm, you may encounter more blocks and barriers in the form of fear and doubt. The closer you come to achieving a goal, you may experience something Maria Nemeth calls "trouble at the border" in her book *The Energy of Money*. "Trouble at the border" occurs when you get closer to moving something from the invisible realm of possibility into the physical realm of reality. This is a natural part of your conscious business evolution and something to welcome with open arms when it happens. Because, it means you are approaching the border, and therefore very close to seeing your dream become real.

If you find yourself struggling with fear or doubt as you approach the reality of your dream, I invite you to consider this: there are no mistakes and you cannot fail. You read that right. There are no mistakes and you cannot fail. Each step you take in the fulfillment of your dreams either leads you towards your goal or teaches you valuable information to know if or when to redirect your plan.

This is called learning in action. It is, by far, the fastest way to learn anything in business or in life. One of my favorite sayings is "you can't steer a parked car." The sooner you get into action, the sooner you will realize if you are on track, or not, and if you need to course correct. You will save more time, money and energy by getting the ball rolling to see what happens rather than procrastinating, planning and perfecting, but never actually doing. This is why I recommend my "sticky note action plan." It's not about perfect planning, it's about making planning fun and something you can easily take strides in implementing.

Your actions are the way in which you show the Universe you are ready for what's next. Approach each action with the openness to receive whatever gifts you are given. I trust many times you'll receive the gift of reassurance by having the Universe fully support your action. Other times you'll receive the gift or wisdom and redirection as you are pointed down your Divine path with deeper understanding and clarity.

Throw Your Book Bag Over The Fence

I often tell my clients to throw their book bag over the fence. Take action, do something. Make a commitment to implement! Once your book bag is tossed over the fence (you commit to action) you've got to go get your book bag (do what you said you'd do).

For those of you who truly find yourself gripped by procrastination, here are a few ways to get your book bag over the fence and implement! Whenever I find myself in this situation (which is less and less these days), I follow one of these two methods to stop procrastinating and get going. But, before you read further, think about one project that's been on your "to do" list for quite a while. Then, after you discover the following two tools, choose one of them to move your project from procrastination to realization.

Make A Financial Commitment

You've probably heard the expression, "Put some skin in the game." The "skin" this phrase refers to is money. So, if you're on the fence about taking action on something, one of the best ways to break your inertia and start moving is to make a financial commitment to your goal. When you've got "skin" in the game, you have a good reason to get going… every DOLLAR is a reason!

For many entrepreneurs, myself included, I invest in a coach to help me achieve my goals. Something happens when you make a financial commitment (to yourself)… you want to get your money's worth! So, if you're the type of person who wants to get YOUR money's worth, invest in a coach whose hourly rate is out of your comfort zone. Stretching beyond your comfort zone is the critical piece in stepping up your own business and ending procrastination.

For some people $50 is a stretch, for others $5,000 is a stretch. Whatever feels like a stretch to you, make that investment, and a commitment to get your money's worth. The results will astound you.

Make A Public Commitment

Another way to end procrastination is to make a public commitment. A public commitment is one where you tell other people what you're going to do, and when you're going to do it. When you have a commitment to other people, the responsibility to "make good" on your word will get you in gear to finally accomplish the project you've been putting off. As a conscious entrepreneur, your integrity is one of your most valuable assets, so this tool can be a good one to get you in action. Do what you say you're going to do!

Here are a few examples of how you can make a public commitment:

- Schedule a seminar you want to teach (and put a deposit down on the room).
- Announce to your ezine subscribers something you're GOING to offer.
- Say "yes" to a speaking engagement before you have the speech written.
- Say "yes" to anything that fits in your business plan... BEFORE you're "ready."
- Pre-sell a product prior to its completion.
- Tell people you're going to do something, and THEN figure out how to do it.

Warning: Public commitments are not for the faint of heart. These types of commitments can be scarier than putting "skin" in the game. If you make a public commitment to stop your procrastination, be prepared to possibly "sweat it out" a few times before it all comes together. On the other hand, this is a GREAT way to get your tush in gear.

Now that you know the top two ways to end procrastination, go back to the task that came to mind at the beginning of this section. Decide which of the above two tools you'll use to end your procrastination and implement once and for all.

Remember, your intentions in the invisible world need to be matched with actions in the visible world, in order to really see results. Be a decisive, action-oriented person who implements... knowing that your action is part of the unfolding of your Divine Plan.

Take Action By Saying "No"

Remember the t-shirts that said, "What part of NO don't you understand?" I used to get a kick every time I saw that t-shirt because I was the type of person who found the word "no" very difficult to say. And, here was someone who wore it proudly on their t-shirt, that they were a person who liked saying no. Thankfully, I've come a long way with regards to the word "no" and while you'll never see me wearing a "no" t-shirt, you will hear me say "no" more often than before. I bring this up to you now, because "no" is considered an action word. In fact, some of the most challenging actions you'll take in your business (and life) will be to say "no" to something, or someone.

But, for many conscious entrepreneurs, your sensitivity and awareness of others as Divine beings, significantly increases the ease in which you say "yes"... and you don't even entertain the thought of saying "no, thank you." It's understandable that you want to help others, and be of service to them, but saying "yes" when you really feel like saying "no" sends conflicting, confusing and unclear messages to the Universe.

So, why does it serve your highest good to say no? Because

every time you say "no" to what you don't want, you're saying "yes" to what you do want. Saying "no" to one thing adds energy to another thing which you desire more of. "No" is a great way to send a clear signal to the Universe. It shows that you're 100% willing to "put your money where your mouth is" and make decisions that support your highest good.

When you take into consideration the plan you've developed for your business, you'll discover that having a plan makes it much easier to know what to say "yes" to and what opportunities to turn down. And, just like any other muscle, the more you exercise your "no" muscle, the easier it is to use.

The biggest barrier you'll face in saying "no" is the fear of letting others down. When that fear leads you, you let yourself down. You're not supposed to do things that don't feel right to you. Remember, your job as a conscious entrepreneur is to keep your emotions and energies up into the higher vibrational realms, and it's impossible to do that if you're always doing things you wish you didn't have to do. So, start saying "no." If it doesn't feel right to say "yes," it's not aligned with your Divine Plan. You'll know when it's the right time to say "yes" because it'll increase your energy, fill your heart with joy and bring a sense of satisfaction to your soul.

So, as you take action and make more commitments, you just may discover that you need to commit to saying "no." You get the idea? "No" is a strategy for giving birth to your business vision.

ACTION GUIDE EXERCISE #16

Write a list of things you need to say "no" to.

www.TheFreedomFormula.com/guide

Make Every Day Count

Now that you know the importance of having a plan, making commitments, ending procrastination, and implementing (even if that means saying 'no'), it's time to take a look at how you can boil this down to the everyday events of your life. After all, those things you choose to do each day are the things that will make up the fabric of your existence.

If you've ever taken a goal setting or time management seminar, you know the importance of writing things down and planning the activity of your days to help you achieve your end goal. I used to be a daily planning junkie. I needed my daily planner almost more than I needed food, water and sleep to survive. If I left home without it, I'd go back home to get it because "my life" was in that planner. It was somewhat of a dysfunction and a joking point among my friends because if they saw me, they saw my maroon leather encased daily planner in hand. In hindsight, I think my hefty daily planner filled with tons of things to do every day was a way for me to boost the low self-esteem I had at that point in my life. I'd not yet discovered the depth of my faith, my spiritual path and my Divine gifts in the world.

Anyway, I was so addicted to daily planning and writing down a gazillion things on my daily "to do" list that I was a very late adapter when it came to going digital with my daily planner. Finally, when I did go digital with a handheld personal device (PDA), it was awesome! It was easier to organize my overflowing "to do" list and feel even more significant because I could easily manage multiple "to do" lists at the touch of a button. Heaven, right?

Not exactly. It wasn't until my electronic planner broke that I realized how much my "to do" list obsession was stopping me from achieving anything. At the end of the day, yes, I could check off a bunch of things on my "to do" list, but they didn't mean anything. Nor, did those items on my list propel me forward toward my goals. They just kept me busy, and feeling very important because I had so much to do. So, when my planner went "ka-put," I decided not to replace it, and I started managing a much smaller "to do" list with much more important tasks. The results? I achieved my goals faster and easier than ever before. I didn't waste time on un-important tasks, I got focused on what really mattered, and what would have the most impact on my business and my life.

Today, my average daily task list has only three items on it. Coming from someone who used to consider anything less than ten items a complete waste of a day, I've made some real progress… and started making what I'd consider some real money, too.

You see, the fewer things you do, the more your energy is focused on a particular result. The more you do, the more scattered your energy. And, scattered energy doesn't send a clear signal to the Universe to support your endeavors. Instead, scattered energy puts the Universe on hold because it doesn't know how to respond to you.

That being said, I encourage you to break your big plan down into daily actions. Each day include only two to three action items that you consider high priority tasks; tasks that give you a sense of accomplishment at the end of the day that you have made progress toward your goals. This strategy, alone, will drastically shift your focus and energy, and as a result, the Universe's ability to favorably respond to you by sending you an abundance of opportunities, and as a result, more money in your bank.

Plan To Take Care Of Yourself

As a 20 year veteran of the fitness industry, I'd be remiss to not take this opportunity to talk with you about planning to take care of yourself. The plans you have for your business, and your life, don't mean anything if you don't have your health.

Your physical well-being contributes to your emotional well-being, which contributes to your spiritual well-being, which contributes to your physical well-being. It's all interconnected. That's one of the great things about being a conscious entrepreneur, you get to look at every aspect of your life and fully integrate it into one unified, integrated life that is lived to its fullest potential.

This is not a fitness book, so I'm not going to be long-winded about you taking care of yourself. But, here are a few general guidelines it's wise to follow in maintaining the health needed to pursue (and enjoy) your dreams.

- Exercise at least three times per week.
- Eat sensible, well-balanced meals.
- Get enough sleep (average person needs 7-8 hours).
- Drink 64 ounces of water per day.
- Reduce intake of soda, caffeine, sugar, processed foods and alcohol.
- Take time to relax and rest (other than sleeping).
- Be proactive about taking charge of your health.

Here are a few of my personal favorites when it comes to maintaining my health:

- Eat an apple a day.
- Cook with whole grains, my favorite is Quinoa.
- Jump on my rebounder (mini-trampoline) for 30 minutes.
- Take my daughter out for a walk in the stroller.
- Go out dancing.
- Practice Yoga.
- Eliminate soda or coffee, I drink herbal tea and naturally flavored seltzer water (no sugar, no additives, great taste).
- Sleep seven to eight hours per night.
- Relieve stress in an aromatherapy bath.
- Escape to the spa once every few months for a day of pampering.
- Get outside as much as possible to enjoy nature.

So, that's all I'm going to say about planning for your health. I trust these few ideas helped confirm that you're already taking good care of your health, or have renewed your commitment to take action toward improving the way in which you love and care for your physical self. Simply keep in mind that you are a spiritual being expressed in the form of a physical body. As a conscious entrepreneur you have an obligation to keep your soul's home in good health, so you can more fully (and more easily) express the ever glowing, ever expanding Divine light within.

Implement, Implement, Implement

The most important concept you need to draw from this chapter is to get into action in the physical, tangible world. Creating and executing your plan, on every level, is your road-map to being everything you are meant to be in the world, doing those things you are destined to be doing and having those things (and experiences) that are divinely meant for you.

Remember, the meditator on the mountain trying to manifest a million dollars never had a bag of money drop on her head. It's imperative you take all of your spiritual understandings and divine aspirations and show the Universe you are serious about seeing them realized. This happens through the actions you take (action is the most powerful form of prayer) and the consciousness/intention you have when taking those actions.

Please do not take this chapter lightly. This is where the rubber hits the road. It's as if you are "pregnant" with your highest and best potential, but until you go through "labor" (implementing your plan), your divine gifts within will not get birthed into the real world. And, as I mentioned earlier, one of the biggest benefits to executing your plan and taking action is the gift of learning in action. So, before you begin the next chapter on realizing your dreams, take a moment to schedule time to focus on your plan and take steps to "birth" your new business vision.

ACTION GUIDE EXERCISE #17

Write down the 5 most important things for you to implement, and the date by which you'll take action.

www.TheFreedomFormula.com/guide

Maintain Your Energy and Realize Your Dreams

(Soul + Connection + Design + Implementation) x Energy = F

The final step to *The Freedom Formula* is the glorious experience of realizing your dreams. This step of the formula is the opposite of the previous chapters on implementing your new business vision. This chapter is about opening yourself up to receive the fruits of your mental, spiritual and physical "labor." We'll cover two primary concepts in this chapter. The first is how to energetically open yourself up to receive your portion of the infinite abundant supply of the Universe. The second is how to help you maintain the highest energy possible to continue your journey of personal transformation, spiritual connection and business success.

Be Open to Receive

For many of us conscious business owners, we're very used to giving, serving and being there for others. Receiving, on the other hand, doesn't come as naturally. To give you an example, recall a moment when you received a genuine compliment from a friend. What did you do? Chances are you down played whatever they acknowledged in you. Compliments are rarely received with a simple, "thank you." There's usually something attached to it to diminish the significance of that which you're being complimented on.

Perhaps it comes from a society that told you, "don't be too full of yourself," "it's not nice to brag," and the list could go on and on. Culturally we are not raised to hold our heads high and say "thank you," I appreciate your acknowledgment and I agree with you. Whatever the reason for this dismissal of receiving compliments doesn't matter. What matters is that you become aware of how you personally stand in this regard and begin accepting compliments in a completely new way.

So, why are we talking about compliments, and how to accept them? Because it's a lesson in Receiving 101. How you receive a compliment is indicative of your overall ability to receive. The next time someone gives you a compliment, whether it's for your fantastic shoes, a stellar speech, or your ability to listen and support, practice simply saying "thank you." And stop there! Do not justify, do not explain how you got the shoes on sale, or didn't really think your speech was very good, or that it was "nothing" to be there for a friend. These are all ways to show the Universe that you are not ready to receive... anything. How can you receive money, love, or fame, whatever you desire, if you can't receive a compliment on your new shoes?! Think about it.

Another fantastic way to exercise your receiving muscle is around the good green stuff. No, not wheat grass... we're talking about money, here! Have you ever done this? You receive a payment for one of your products or services, and rather than expressing your deepest gratitude for receiving the money (even if it's only $20) you dismiss the money with an instant thought of how it's not enough. Well, what kind of message are you sending to the Universe when you do this? How can you expect to attract thousands of dollars, perhaps millions of dollars, if you have no appreciation for $20?

I can only share this with you because I've been guilty of this myself. There have been times when I would attract even thousands of dollars, and the first thought in my mind was, "it's not enough, I need more." Rather than, "thank you!" It was like a magnet with a negative force that repelled money away from me. And it will for you, too. I've even learned to stop and pick up pennies I see lying on the ground (thanks to T. Harv Eker), with the awareness that those pennies remind me to acknowledge my gratitude for receiving even the smallest amount of money.

So, now I ask you to take an honest assessment of how you receive money. Do you receive $1,000 differently than $10? What do you need to do to have the same feeling of gratitude no matter what the amount is? This is your exercise. Begin looking for pennies on the ground, and picking them up with a feeling of gratitude, as if it's a "God wink" especially for you. If you receive checks, when you endorse them write the words "thank you" on the check. Chellie Campbell taught me this strategy several years ago, and it works.

If you have an Internet based business and you never physically hold the money, but simply see a receipt that a deposit has been made to your bank account, take a moment, when you get the receipt, to acknowledge receiving that money as if it were handed to you. You can simply say the words "thank you" out loud as if you were talking directly to God for sending the money to you. If you'd like you can add a statement like this, "I gratefully receive the money you have sent to me. I acknowledge this money as a Divine gift and accept it with joy and gratitude." Notice the difference between this statement and the words, "It's not enough, I need more." Now, make a conscious choice to appreciate every dollar (every penny) that you receive. And, trust that the Universe hears you loud and clear.

Once you embrace receiving compliments and money, you will find it easier to identify so many other things you can express gratitude for receiving. To help, here are a few of my favorite gifts to exercise my receiving muscle:

- A "world famous" hug from my daughter
- A gentle breeze caressing my face
- Morning cuddles with my husband
- A "just called to say Hi" conversation with a friend
- A thank you note from a client
- No line at the grocery store
- Reading just the right article at just the right time
- Someone letting me into a lane of traffic
- Hearing the word "yes" when I ask for help

Begin looking at your life through the eyes of receiving. The more you authentically express gratitude for receiving, the more you will be given. Receiving is like a receptacle that gets bigger and bigger the more you consciously receive.

Action Guide Exercise #18

Write a list of at least 25 'gifts' you are grateful for receiving.

www.TheFreedomFormula.com/guide

Eventually, you'll experience the feeling of your "cup runneth over" because you'll begin receiving so much, your Self and your business need to catch up with all that you are receiving. Which brings me to the next point.

How to Manage Growth

As a conscious entrepreneur, one of the goals for your business is growth. The more your business grows, the more people you serve, the more lives you impact, the more you contribute to the positive evolution of the world. But, here's where many conscious business owners fall short. They limit their growth to what they think they can manage. Why? Growth can be scary sometimes. You begin to deal with hiring and management issues... even if you outsource everything to independent contractors. You may experience cash flow issues because a lot of money is going toward supporting the growth of your business. You may fear you'll be hand-cuffed to your laptop, working nights and weekends and missing out on the rest of life and family.

All of these above mentioned growth concerns are good for you, and your business. If you are faced with growth issues, it means you are doing a great job of receiving, and attracting that which you have always desired. Business growth is an individualized crash course in priorities, asking for help, knowing when to say "no," and everything else you've learned about in this book. Growth is the result of living the four components of a conscious business. Growth is what conscious business is all about! Growth… and the impact it has on the world.

So, as you expand your receiving mechanism, and appreciate everything that comes to you, it's important that you simultaneously plan for the growth of your business. Begin asking for help, before you need it. Investigate legal and tax issues associated with growth so you are prepared for them when needed. My husband and I just recently took a big step in this area and it feels amazing. We met with an estate attorney to set up our trusts, wills and guardian papers for our daughter. This was not an easy task to do. But, for us, it felt like a necessary step to take with the growth that's occurring in my business. It was my way of showing the Universe I was serious about my business, serious about making a lot of money, and serious about protecting my family and my assets as that growth occurs. This was an action that made me expand my receiving capacity even more. I was preparing myself and my family to receive so much more than we had up to this point.

One other action I recommend you take in receiving and preparing for growth is to begin setting up your conscious business to run without you. That's not a typo. Your business should be set up to run without you. I'm not saying your business *should* run without you, but it ought to be able to. If you're the only person who knows the inner workings of your business, growth will bring you much headache, and heartache. On the other hand, if you take the necessary steps to put systems in place, to train your team to take over if needed, to get the knowledge in your head onto paper and transferred to others, you again send a strong message to the Universe that you're ready to receive more and that you're ready for rapid, expansive growth.

If you're looking for a resource to help you systematize your business operations in a way that is easy and that works, I highly recommend my friend and colleague Beth Schneider (who helped me with my systems) at **www.ProcessProdigy.com**

You see, when you are committed to being a conscious entrepreneur, you cannot ignore any aspect of your business, or your life. Nothing can be swept under the carpet. Consciousness is about the awareness of it all and the willingness to act according to your awareness and the alignment of what you see in your present life and what you envision for your future life. This might sound like hard work; to be aware of every aspect of your life, looking at it all with wide open eyes and taking responsibly and doing something about it. The truth is, if you think it's hard work, it will be. On the other hand, if you accept your conscious business responsibilities as the most valuable Divine gift you could ever ask for, you'll discover this way of living is easy, and you'll experience the Divine in every moment, even when the moment feels challenging.

Next, you'll discover how to design environments that support your success and help you maintain your highest energy. Environments shape your reality, and can help you more easily (and lovingly) move through the challenging times. Taking responsibility as a conscious entrepreneur is not a walk in the park; it takes discipline in spirit, mind, heart and body to maintain this path. Environments have everything to do with your ability to stay energized and continue putting one foot in front of the other.

Environments Create Your Reality

Environments are critically important to your conscious business success because they help you maintain a higher vibration. The more positive energy you are able to hold (feeling good as opposed to feeling bad, seeing the cup half full rather than half empty) the more ease and joy you will experience on your journey. And, the more ease and joy you experience, the more the feelings of ease and joy increase.

We talked about this in an earlier chapter as it pertains to the concept of "what you think about, you bring about." Environments have much to do with the thoughts that pass through your mind, consciously and unconsciously. With the conscious awareness of setting up environments to support you, you can have a drastic positive influence on your state of being... the place from which all things manifest. So, let's look at the different types of environments and how you can use them to support your highest, Divine good to keep the energy flowing!

Environment is broken down into two categories. Internal and external. Internal environments include your mindset, attitudes, connection with God, sense of peace, beliefs, faith and level of trust. These are all environments that exist within you, and can be affected by your external environments. Granted, internal environments are not exclusively reliant on external environments, just think of Nelson Mandela and you know what I'm talking about here. But, let's not set an intention that you strengthen your inner environment by facing extraordinary challenges in the external world.

Instead, here we're going to focus on setting up supportive, loving, uplifting external environments that infuse you with energy.

Of course, the very fact that you have a conscious business is one tremendous environment right there. But, there are many more environments that can be designed to support your ultimate success. Some of these have already been mentioned in other parts of this book, but for the sake of making it easy for you to have one complete resource at your finger tips, here are the environments I've used that have been a great success for me. I trust you'll resonate with at least one of them and get to work implementing it in your life right away. Remember, this final step of *The Freedom Formula* is about maintaining your energy and receiving your dreams. These external environments are designed to help you do just that.

Physical Surroundings

The physical surroundings that you exist in every day in your home, office, and car are environments that have a massive impact on you. Why? Because they are the literal environments in which everything else occurs. If you are surrounded by clutter, stacks and stacks of papers that need to be filed, have bookcases that look they belong in the thrift store and a bathroom that hasn't been cleaned in weeks... these are all examples of environments that do not contribute to your highest and best good.

When you exist in less than desirable environments, a messy car for example, the feeling you have as you sit behind the wheel is pulled down because the space that surrounds you doesn't represent that Divine spark within. I'm not saying that you need to live in a big home, with new furniture, drive a fancy car and hire a professional organizer. What I am saying is it's your responsibility to take care of those possessions you have (everything from your home to the papers in your file drawer) in a way that supports you to be your best.

Sometimes this will mean you give away furniture, eliminate old files that have no relevance anymore, donate a bunch of old clothes to a charity, get your car washed, or hire a housekeeper to keep your home clean. I know you know what I'm talking about here. Just think about the last time you organized a drawer, cleaned out a closet, or gave your car a detail job. Feels great, doesn't it? Because you've released stagnant, cluttered energy that was making you feel stagnant and confused; it gave you more energy.

I've got one word of caution when it comes to physical environments. Do not take everything on at once. If you think of organizing and de-cluttering your entire office, it can feel too overwhelming to start. Instead, begin with one drawer, not even the whole desk. One drawer at a time, one file at a time, you will slowly but surely begin to experience a physical environment that actually supports you in achieving your goals.

Accountability Buddy

An accountability buddy is a trusted friend or colleague who cares about you, your business and your life, but different than a visioning partner. Once you've identified that person, simply set up a phone call with him or her every week, preferably at the same time each week. Ten minutes is all you need to schedule with your buddy.

When you hop on the phone with each other you simply state those tasks which you are committed to doing that week, those tasks you intended to accomplish the past week, and a status report of whether or not you did what you said you were going to do. You both write down what you're committed to doing the following week, and you write down what your buddy is committed to doing, too. That way, the next week when you talk, you can hold them accountable and not let them slip any undone commitments through the cracks. This is about holding each other to a standard of honesty and integrity in achieving your goals.

With that in mind, you do not have permission to beat

yourself up, or your buddy up if they do not honor their commitment. Rather, take a look at the commitment and identify what happened that it was not realized. Maybe it becomes insignificant in the course of your week, maybe a fear came up around doing it, and maybe you simply pro-crastinated. Whatever it is, identify the reason why and either re-commit to doing it, or remove it from your task list for the coming week, if it no longer serves you to accomplish it. This pertains to the section where we discussed "dumping" tasks that are no longer aligned with you. Never do something just because you said you would, if it no longer resonates with you as something worth doing.

Keep in mind that these tasks you commit to doing each week are designed to infuse you with energy and help you be your highest and best Divine expression in the world. If they're not connected to that end goal, they are worth some serious consideration if you should be doing them at all, or perhaps delegating them to someone else to do.

Vision Partner

A vision partner is set up similarly to an accountability buddy, except what you discuss each week when you talk is com-pletely different. A vision partner is someone who holds a space for you to verbally communicate the vision that is in your heart and soul. The vision can relate to your conscious business, your life, your relationships, the dreams you want to manifest, vacations you want to take, anything that tickles your fancy and evokes an energized state of being. Having a vision partner to receive your vision and believe it for you (remember, they're seeing it as already done) is one of the most powerful and fun tools you have to boost your level of energy, enthusiasm and anticipation of what's yet to be revealed.

When working with your vision partner, it helps to create a physical environment to support the conversation. Light a candle, play some relaxing music, dim the lights, allow yourself to physically relax and take a few deep breaths. Creating this sacred spaced in which to share your vision contributes to the energy which is released as you speak.

Each of you in the vision partner relationship has an obligation to listen to your partner without judgment. You simply open your heart and mind to receive what they have to share as if it's an absolutely already done deal. Then, it's even more amazing to hear of the visions that you shared being realized.

Mastermind Group

A mastermind group generally consists of two or more people who gather (in person or via telephone) for the sole purpose of supporting each other. There is no particular leader, each person in the group shows up as a leader for each other. No one is "in charge" in a mastermind group. It's an environment that allows for you to ask for support, resources, input and ideas for any challenges you may be facing in your conscious business. This group should consist of trusted, like-minded, respected colleagues who you are eager to contribute to, and who have an equal contribution to offer you.

A mastermind group typically meets weekly or monthly and has more of a back and forth flow than the astute listening that transpires in an accountability buddy or vision partner relationship. This is where you get to bat around ideas with your equals, and receive valuable solutions, wisdom, insight and support.

I personally participate in three different Mastermind groups via telephone. One that meets once per week, one that meets twice per month and one that meets once per month. All of them are invaluable environments in my life that are huge sources of support in the pursuit of my business (and life) goals. To know that I have trusted colleagues to connect with and to help me on a consistent, on-going basis is a gift beyond words.

Circle Community

A circle community is like a spiritually focused mastermind, and occurring generally once per month in person. In a circle, the leadership rotates from gathering to gathering. So, everyone is seen as equals and steps up to share leadership responsibility. The agenda for a circle remains consistent from month to month, and includes an opening/centering, sharing tool and closing.

Women's circles, specifically, have been around since the cave days where women gathered in circle around the camp fire to support each other in their lives... mostly supporting each other to stay alive in those times. In today's environment, women's circles are popping up in every corner of the world, for the sole purpose of supporting each of it's participants in their highest good, and the highest good of the world.

For me, personally, my circles are one of the most influential and all-sustaining environments I have in my life. I strongly encourage you to take a look at **www.CircleGuidebook.com** if you have an interest in starting your own circle. Don't worry guys, a circle can also include or be exclusively made up of men.

Relationships

This external environment doesn't need much explaining. You know if the relationships in your life are serving you, or not. The ones that serve you, infuse you with energy and cause you to have "woo-hoo" moments. They are the relationships that you leave feeling so much better than before you interacted with that person.

On the other hand, relationships that don't serve you feel like someone is sucking the life out of you. They drain you, draw from your light and leave you feeling frustrated, discouraged, or just plain tired. Do your best to limit these depleting, draining relationships and develop relationships with those people who support you, believe in you and celebrate you!

Coaching Circle

Coaching circles are becoming more and more popular and range in their level of involvement. A coaching circle has one specific designated leader, who is paid to be the environment for the clients he or she has attracted to be in their circle. Some coaches offer these circles in the form of a monthly membership program that includes ongoing learning opportunities, resources, tips and tools exclusively made available only to those people who are members of their circle. In this type of external environment, you may be one of 25 members or one of 250 members, or more. It's a scalable business for the coach who facilitates the coaching circle and each person, no matter how many join the circle, gets the same level of service as everyone else.

Other coaching circles are more intimate, limited only to a dozen people or so. These type of circles cost a lot more money than the type I just mentioned because there is a lot more one-on-one involvement between the coach and the members of the circle. Live, face-to-face facilitated meetings are one of the most valuable aspects to these more intimate, supportive environments.

The good thing about coaching circles is that there is one for every budget. Whether you've got $50 per month or $5,000 per month to invest in a circle, there are a plethora of options for you to choose from to get involved in this type of environment.

Of course, I hope you'll take advantage of your 30-day FREE trial in my Conscious Business Circle and join hundreds of members who consistently reap the rewards of interacting with me on a regular basis. Visit **www.ConsciousBusinessCircle.com** to join today.

Coaching Group

A coaching group is a smaller group that meets in person or via telephone usually for a specific purpose and a designated amount of time. It consists of people who pay to be in the coaching group because they want to learn from that specific coach who will help them individually and collectively achieve their topic-specific goals.

Some people join coaching groups to help them create information products, establish their brand, create a website, learn how to implement a publicity campaign, discover how to invest in real estate, how to improve their relationships, or in my case, to help Get Your Book Done™ or fully implement *The Freedom Formula* into your life. The options are as endless as there are coaches with information and expertise that helps others.

To learn more about my coaching programs, please visit **www.LoveYourLife.com**

Private Coach

A private coach is someone you hire to work one-on-one with you, and only you. This type of coaching requires more of a financial investment, because the coach is making him or herself more available to you. They'll give you an individualized approach to reach your specific goals and are an amazing resource to connect you with everything you need to achieve your goals.

Private coaching formats range from a 30 minute phone

conversation every week to private full-day or weekend retreats and year-long intensives. And, the price tags range according to the programs. Often, conscious entrepreneurs make this type of investment in a specific coach because they know that coach has wisdom and information that can help them multiply their investment several times over.

If you are looking for someone who is dedicated to your success, will push you, ask you the hard questions, share their wisdom generously, and who you have a heart/soul connection with, then a private coach is the perfect external environment to help you achieve your goals and more.

If you're interested in working with me privately please email **info@LoveYourLife.com** to request a private coaching application.

ACTION GUIDE EXERCISE #19

Make a commitment to the environments you'll put in place to support you. What do you need to change, take away, or add?

www.TheFreedomFormula.com/guide

It Takes a Village

You've heard the expression, "It takes a village to raise a child." I take this phrase one step further to say, "It takes a village to raise a conscious entrepreneur." Any dream worth pursuing can't be done alone. You'll need help along the way; for moral support, a shoulder to cry on, cheerleaders to celebrate your greatest victories, people to share their wisdom and resources with you and to believe in you if ever you lose belief in yourself. Your "village" is there to keep you on track to manifest everything your heart desires (this or something better, right?). I once heard someone say there are no self-made millionaires; anyone who has made a million dollars made it by having a "village" of support, a team.

Getting support is what gives me the energy I need to take some major risks in my business, do things I never thought I could do, dream bigger than I used to dream, and keep going when it feels impossible. Having a support network around you will literally make the difference between success and failure, between a $50,000 business and a $500,000 business (or more), between just getting by and as Oprah would say, "Living your best life!"

Maintain the Process

One of the most important things to remember on your journey of putting soul in your business and money in your bank is to stay in the process. The life of a conscious entrepreneur requires a lot of emotional, spiritual and physical energy. So, if you ever become complacent, lazy, tired, disengaged from the greater good of the universe or unenthused about evolving, transforming and growing, it's time to put at least one of the previously listed external environments into place to make sure you stay in the process.

And, here's a bit of encouragement for those moments you do feel disconnected and disengaged in the Divine Unfolding of your life. The simple fact that you recognize when you are disconnected is proof that you *are* connected. In recognizing the absence of connection, you make yourself aware of connection. It is the awareness of the absence that brings forth the sense of presence, and engagement in your Divine path.

Another thing to always keep in mind as you experience the ups and downs of the conscious evolution of you and your business is that it's impossible to fail. Anything that feels like failure isn't; it's simply a lesson offering guidance for what actions to take next. It shows you one way things didn't work out as hoped and therefore points you closer to what will work out as you envision.

Imagine yourself on a hike and you come to a fork in the trail. You're not sure which way to go so you choose one of your two options only to realize you made the wrong choice. Now, it's true, you went out of your way a bit and "failed" to make the right choice, but the good news is now you know exactly where to go because one of your two options didn't work out.

Keep this analogy in mind for your business. You will make plenty of turns that lead you down a path that isn't the "right" path. But, each path you take, and each one that isn't "right" is there to serve your highest good, teach you valuable lessons, offer valuable insights, bring you new relationships, new ideas and a blinking signpost as to where you ought to be going next. Well, that road didn't work out, so you have a new opportunity to make a different choice. You simply cannot fail when you accept that failure doesn't exist; it's a disguise for the gifts of guidance, wisdom, insight, deepened faith and personal transformation.

Persistence is Power

Conscious entrepreneurship requires persistence. As with any aspiration in life giving up doesn't serve anyone, especially you. If you are committed to living the four components of conscious business; making money, making a difference, being fully who you are and trusting in your Divine path… quitting isn't an option. Let me rephrase that.

Quitting those things that no longer serve the highest expression of your Divine self is a good thing. But, quitting on the pursuit of your highest self-expression isn't. Right? I quit one of my businesses because it was a considerable drain on my time, money and energy. But, quitting on that business was a necessary action in order for me to stay committed to my highest self. That business was weighing me down. Without it, I've been able to soar so much higher than I ever would have if I had kept it open.

Persistence can be a tricky thing. You can persist forever trying to push a piece of string uphill. And, no matter how long you try, how much you intend and envision pushing that string up hill, the fact is that you can't push a string uphill. It's physically impossible. If you find yourself pushing a string uphill, do not persist. Put your heart, soul and energy into a more fulfilling endeavor, one that has true potential for extraordinary results on every level of your existence.

The highest endeavor to pursue is connecting more and more closely with God, and with the expression of that Divine spark within, through the gift of your business. This is the kind of persistence I'm talking about. And, persistence in the pursuit of experiencing God's greatest good is the best kind of persistence in the world.

The more frequently and more consistently you maintain your conscious connection to Source and take action based on your highest Divine self, the more trust you will have in yourself and the Divine order of your life.

Everything is this chapter is geared toward keeping your energy up, to keeping the "positive vibes" flowing through you in each and every moment. Energy allows for receiving. Receiving gives you energy. It is the continuous cycle of a conscious entrepreneur. Energy is the MULTIPLIER of *The Freedom Formula* so please do whatever it takes to maintain your emotional, spiritual and physical energy.

I talked a lot about outside support in this chapter. Outside support is something it took me a long time to embrace. I thought I had to do everything on my own. I'm not sure what it is about us humans but for some reason, we are afraid to ask for help. Some people think it is a sign of weakness. I see it as a sign of great strength. It takes courage to open yourself up to the "village" and be accountable to a coach or mastermind group or partner. But courage moves you through fear and draws you further along your journey of freedom.

Freedom Revisited

The ultimate entrepreneurial dream is freedom. The pursuit of which invites you to face your fears, expand your vision, get way out of your comfort zone and open up to let Source guide you to your highest and richest expression in the world.

Think back to the beginning of this book, where I asked you to write your personal definition of freedom? Do you remember your definition? Did you want to be free from something that was weighing you down? Did you want freedom to pursue something? Whether you wanted to be free *from* something or free to move *toward* something, freedom as it pertains to conscious entrepreneurship is a process of putting all the pieces of *The Freedom Formula* together.

It is to discover the Soul in your business, and connect with your Source as well as your market. It is about designing and implementing your business vision by taking action on your plan (remember the old adage: failing to plan is planning to fail). And, it is about maintaining your energy to receive and realize your dreams. Yes, there are many aspects to consider when putting soul in your business and money in your bank, but the good news is you now have the formula to make it all possible. I invite you to use this formula to experience the ultimate success in your business and your life... freedom!

$$(Soul + Connection + Design + Implementation)$$
$$x\ Energy = FREEDOM$$

ACTION GUIDE EXERCISE #20

Revisit your personal definition of freedom and see if your definition needs to be shifted now after completing this book.

www.TheFreedomFormula.com/guide

Congratulations… you did it! Now, enjoy LIVING it!

A F T E R W O R D

The End is the Beginning

Take a look at the five steps of *The Freedom Formula* again:

- Step 1: Discover the Soul in Your Business
- Step 2: Connect to Your Source... and to Your Market
- Step 3: Design Your Business
- Step 4: Implement Your Business Vision
- Step 5: Maintain Your Energy and Realize Your Dreams

Once you complete the fifth step of maintaining your energy and realizing your dreams, you may find yourself naturally cycling back to the beginning... and re-discovering the soul in your business at your new level of success.

You see, as a conscious entrepreneur, your journey never ends until your spirit leaves your physical body. As long as you are a living, breathing creature of God walking on this earth in this incarnation, your journey will never end. Every day brings new opportunity, new insights, new understanding, new relationships, new ideas, new businesses, new approaches... new everything.

It's about the journey, not the destination. Your responsibility now is to surrender to the journey of your conscious business, as a pure and sacred expression of who you Divinely are. And, I mean ALL of who you are. No part of your being gets to hide, no part of you gets to dim its light. Every part of you needs to be present in every moment.

Please, always continue to pursue your freedom in knowingness that once you experience a new freedom, it is a time of joyous celebration and gratitude for Spirit leading you there. But, truly the greatest gift in the pursuit (and acquisition of your goals) is who you become along the way, moment by moment, experience by experience, and transformation by transformation.

I've designed this book for you so it has value in reading it more than once. You can pick this book up again and again at any point in the future and have a completely new experience in reading it. Because, the eyes in which you'll read these words next year will be different than those you see with today.

AN INVITATION
FROM CHRISTINE

FREE 30-Day membership in my Conscious Business Circle

"I believe that continual learning and implementing are critical elements to your conscious business success. That's why I'm inviting you to learn from me FREE for 30 days in my Conscious Business Circle… and be inspired to take action every single day!"
~ CHRISTINE KLOSER

The Conscious Business Circle is your **one-stop resource to get everything you need** to enjoy a purpose-driven, profitable business and a soul-satisfying life!

The Conscious Business Circle connects conscious entrepreneurs with **tips, tools, strategies,** resources and inspiration to **manifest** a mega-successful, conscious business…. with more **ease, grace and joy**!! This monthly membership program is guaranteed to help you **focus** on your priorities, **connect** to your big vision, **create** your action plan for success and stay on the **cutting-edge** of business and marketing strategies… consciously!

Get your FREE 30-Day membership now!

www.ConsciousBusinessCircle.com.

I look forward to seeing you in "the circle."

To your success,

Christine

Christine Kloser
Author, *The Freedom Formula*

Do You Have Friends, Family or Colleagues that Would Benefit From Reading *The Freedom Formula?*

RECEIVE <u>5 FREE</u> COPIES TO SHARE!

Let's face it! It's a lot easier to pursue and achieve your dreams when you have people around you who believe and live by the same principles as you do. Nothing is worse than sharing your dream with someone, only to have them tell you all the reasons why it's not going to happen and you're crazy for thinking "that" way.

On the other hand, when your friends and colleagues are aligned with you and believe in your dreams – and their own dreams too—there's an energy that fuels you to keep going, no matter what. Your supportive network becomes your insurance policy to never, ever quit your journey of entrepreneurial freedom.

I want to make it EASY for you to share *The Freedom Formula* with your friends and colleagues, so you ALL experience more success, joy and ease... while you put soul in your business and money in your bank.

So, here's the deal:

Buy 5 Copies of *The Freedom Formula* - Get 5 Copies FREE!

That's right... you receive 10 copies for the price of 5! So you can share them with your 10 closest friends, colleagues and clients. This offer is only available to people who have read *The Freedom Formula* by going to this private website:

www.TheFreedomFormula.com/5free

Just in case you're asking yourself why I'm discounting the price 50%.... the answer is simple. For me, this book is about spreading the message of *The Freedom Formula* with conscious entrepreneurs around the world. This book is for your transformation, the transformation of those you care about and the positive transformation of our world.

Thank you in advance for sharing *The Freedom Formula* with those you love.

F R E E   R E S O U R C E S

How to Avoid the Three Massive Mistakes Made by Most Conscious Entrepreneurs!

If you consider yourself a conscious entrepreneur and want to learn how to avoid the pitfalls along the journey and experience success, you'll want to download this FREE special report. It's part of my Conscious Business Success Kit at **www.LoveYourLife.com** - simply enter your name and email on the right side of the homepage.

Conscious Business Connection Newsletter

Interested in learning valuable tips, tools, inspiration and strategies for your soulful success? *Conscious Business Connection* is Christine's FREE newsletter delivered every other Tuesday via email. Visit **www.LoveYourLife.com** to start your complimentary subscription as part of your FREE Conscious Business Success Kit. Simply enter your name and email on the right side of the homepage.

7 Strategies Entrepreneurial Authors Need to Know... Before Writing a Word

Do you have dreams of writing a book to grow your business and share your transformational message with the world? Most conscious entrepreneurs do. But, knowing how to get your book done can be very tricky (the industry sadly has some "unconscious" entrepreneurs). Download this audio as part of Christine's FREE Conscious Business Success Kit to take your first step toward publishing success. Visit **www.LoveYourLife.com** and enter your name and email on the right side of the homepage.

CONTACT
CHRISTINE KLOSER

ADDRESS:
Love Your Life, LLC
PO Box 2
Dallastown, PA 17313

PHONE:
(800) 930-3713

EMAIL:
info@LoveYourLife.com

MAIN WEBSITE:
www.LoveYourLife.com

OTHER WEBSITES:
www.TheFreedomFormula.com
www.FreedomFormulaMovie.com
www.ConsciousBusinessCircle.com
www.LoveYourLifeBooks.com

CONNECT WITH ME ONLINE:
www.ChristineFacebook.com
www.LoveYourLife.com/blog

For quantity discounts, promotions or sponsorship of *The Freedom Formula*, please call (800) 930-3713 ext. 1.

ABOUT THE AUTHOR

Christine Kloser is an inspirational business coach, engaging speaker, award-winning book publisher and author of *The Freedom Formula: How to Put Soul in Your Business and Money in Your Bank*, *Conscious Entrepreneurs: A Radical New Approach to Purpose, Passion and Profit* and the *Inspiration to Realization* book series. Since 1991 she has been an entrepreneur; continually exploring new ways to integrate her spiritual understandings with strategic business tactics for herself and her clients. She provides lectures, training, coaching and book publishing services to thousands of entrepreneurs worldwide.

Named the Wealthy Woman's Business Ambassador for her dedication to empowering women entrepreneurs, Christine has been nationally recognized as a business and empowerment expert. In addition to her own books, her business and success advice has been featured in the books:

- *The Ugly Truth about Small Business* by Ruth King
- *Web Wonder Women* by Lynne Klippel
- *What No One Ever Tells You About Starting Your Own Business* by Jan Norman

- *Empowering Women to Power Network* by Ponn M. Sabra
- *Heart of a Woman* by Sheryl Rousch
- *Secrets of the Millionaire Mind* by T. Harv Eker

A former television host, columnist and seasoned interviewer, Christine has appeared on numerous radio and television programs and has been featured in *Entrepreneur Magazine*, the *Los Angeles Times, The Portland Press* and *Woman's Day*. Her insights and articles are regularly published in her FREE *Conscious Business Connection* ezine, which reaches thousands of conscious entrepreneurs worldwide.

Originally from Connecticut (and 14 years in Los Angeles), Christine now enjoys the expansive views and fresh air in Pennsylvania with her husband, daughter and Schumper, the family cat.

Quick Order Form

Fax: (310) 496-0716
Phone: (800) 930-3713 (have your credit card ready)
Online: www.TheFreedomFormula.com
Postal: Love Your Life, LLC
           PO Box 2, Dallastown, PA 17313

Please send the following books.

_____ copies of *The Freedom Formula®* ($19.95)

Name: _____

Address: _____

City: _____

State: _____ Zip: _____

Telephone: _____

Email: _____

Sales tax: Please add 6% sales tax for products shipped to PA.

SHIPPING:
US: $4.60 For the first book and $1 for each additional book
International: $11.00 For first book and $6 For each additional book

Payment: ☐Check ☐Visa ☐MasterCard ☐Discover ☐Amex

Card Number: _____

Name on Card: _____

Expiration Date: _____

3 or 4 digit CID: _____

Signature: _____